HOW TO BE

Meditation in Spirit and Practice

CLAUDIO NARANJO

JEREMY P. TARCHER, INC.
Los Angeles

Library of Congress Cataloging in Publication Data

Naranjo, Claudio
    How to be / Claudio Naranjo.
        p. cm.
    Rev. and enl. ed. of: On the psychology of meditation. 1971.
    Includes biographical references.
    1. Meditation—Psychology. I. Naranjo, Claudio. On the psychology of
meditation. II. Title.
BL627.N37   1990   89-38263
158 ' .12—dc20   CIP
ISBN 0-87477-548-5

Jeremy P. Tarcher, Inc.
5858 Wilshire Blvd.
Los Angeles, CA 90036

Distributed by St. Martin's Press, New York

Manufactured in the United States of America
10   9   8   7   6   5   4   3   2   1

First Edition

How to Be

CONTENTS

Preface

The first four chapters in this book originally formed a work entitled "Meditation: Its Spirit and Techniques." It was first published in 1971 by Viking Press in a volume entitled *On the Psychology of Meditation* alongside a companion work by Robert Ornstein called "The Techniques of Meditation and Their Implications for Modern Psychology."

I am very pleased with Jeremy Tarcher's initiative in republishing what I wrote on meditation twenty years ago in response to Dr. Ornstein's invitation to coauthor *On the Psychology of Meditation*, which has now been out of print for some time.

At the time I wrote my contribution to that book, I had barely embarked on the path of practice. Now, it has seemed fitting to append to that earlier writing something that reflects my present understanding and experience on the subject.

A first reformulation on the underlying dimensions and processes in the realm of meditation appeared in *Consciousness and Culture* (vol. 1, no. 1) in 1977, and a brief overview of the model presented here was shared at the Bombay meeting of the International Transpersonal Association in 1982. However, the current exposition of my views, "For a Theory of Meditation: An Update," was taken from a talk given in 1984 at the Frankfurt Museum of Natural Sciences under the sponsorship of the Frankfurter Ring.

There is some redundancy between "For a Theory of Meditation" and the essay that follows it, "The Interface between Meditation and Psychotherapy." I have employed the sixfold view in the former as an analytical tool to bear on the issue of the meditation/psychotherapy interface, which is the theme of the latter. The stimulus for the second essay was an invitation to deliver the keynote address at the Conference on Meditation and Psychotherapy, held in Tuscany in October 1988 under the sponsorship of the Siena Gestalt Association and the Rajneesh Miasto.

The third and last addition to this volume, "Music and Meditation as Therapy," was specifically prompted by the prospect of this new publication. As one who stopped writing music at the time of entering medical school and who has been kept away from active musicianship by competing interests and needs, it is not surprising that I developed throughout life alternative avenues of expression for my musical self, one of those being an ongoing exploration of ways of working on consciousness through music. The emphasis throughout these pages on the deliberate use of music for the evocation of sacredness and on the relatively undiscovered healing potential of Brahms' music echoes my emphasis as a psychotherapist and teacher.

In addition to reflection on the essence of meditation and involvement in the application of meditation to psychotherapy, the application of music to spiritual development and healing stands out as a spontaneous direction of specialization throughout my life. As a whole, these three essays—brief as they are—reflect my chief contributions to the understanding and practice of meditation.

I hope the work of synthesis that this book reflects may serve as a catalyst to the ongoing integration of experience in the minds of its readers, and that it may inspire meditation at a time when inwardness holds a promise not only on an individual basis but in view of our social predicament.

Claudio Naranjo
Berkeley, California
January 1990

Introduction

The time when East and West meet, our time, is one of meeting between religions, philosophies, and psychological schools that had hitherto ignored one another or looked upon one another with fanatical disdain. Furthermore, it is a time of meeting between science and religion, psychotherapy and education, a time when we envision the rise of the discipline of integral growth.

Increased ease in communication and cultural openness coincide with awakening of spiritual thirst. Perhaps because of dissatisfaction with and detachment from cultural forms that answered to man's yearning in the past, perhaps because of a measure of disappointment in the ultimate fruits of scientific and technological progress, an increasing number of people are becoming concerned with the question of personal development. An age of self-satisfaction is over, and we have entered an age of seeking.

In our search we look for new answers, but we also turn a respectful gaze to the wisdom of the remote past and to the wisdom of the East that we once thought obsolete and superseded. The extent of generalized interest in the spiritual traditions of Asia may be appreciated in the numerous books in the field that are published month after month, and in the establishment in Europe and in America of Eastern schools—Lamaist monasteries, Zendos, yogi ashramas, Sufi circles.

One particular and concrete instance of the newly awakened search is the rediscovery of meditation. According to an estimate of 1968, more than two thousand students were involved in meditation on the Berkeley campus alone, at the University of California. Numerous seminars or courses in meditation are being offered in the main cultural centers of the United States, mostly by yogis and Zen or Ch'an masters, and by persons like myself who are attempting to pour old wine in new bottles.

In spite of the wealth of information now available to the interested individual, one thing is lacking: a spirit of synthesis. The would-be meditator reads or hears about Zen meditation, about Christian meditation, about yogic practices, and feels that at some level all these are interrelated; but he cannot articulate what it is that these ways have in common, and he may be perplexed or disoriented by the discrepancies. Each way or tradition often claims to be the true one or the most effective. Even the worthiest representatives of a particular school do not generally go beyond a tolerant regard for other schools; they are too steeped in their own traditions to grasp the common root of all systems. Therefore, in this book I have pursued a threefold goal:

1. To explore the unity of spirit or attitude in the multiplicity of ways of meditation—*i.e.*, what meditation is *beyond* its forms.

2. To attempt a general classification of meditation techniques, not in terms of their cultural origin but in terms of their psychological nature.

3. To underline the nature of the psychological processes involved in meditation—processes that constitute the essence and goal of the practice and yet are not evident from the descriptions of the techniques.

The process of trying to understand the common denominator of meditation beyond seemingly different techniques results, I think, in the realization that meditation itself is not something separate or even different from other things. Perhaps this happens with every great idea: once we delve into its substance, we find that it is but one more name of a unity of which it is but one aspect or name. My own exploration of meditation shows me that the essence of meditation is also the essence of art, the essence of religion, the essence of true magic, the essence of psychotherapy, the essence of doing anything in the right attitude. I believe that to a meditator with the right understanding all life is meditation, and meditation is living.

I have not attempted to show in detail the relationships between meditation and other relevant practices, such as movement disciplines[1]* or some forms of psychotherapy,[2] but have indicated enough of the connections between the different ways of meditation and other activities to show that there is a common psychological ground in such seemingly disparate cultural manifestations as shamanism, the rise of moral injunctions, artistic vocation, prophecy, ritual—and meditation. Many fingers pointing at the same target from different directions will designate their object better than one or two.

*Numbered reference notes begin on page *164*.

1 / The Domain of Meditation

The word "meditation" has been used to designate a variety of practices that differ enough from one another so that we may find trouble in defining what *meditation* is.

Is there a commonality among the diverse disciplines alluded to by this same word? Something that makes them only different forms of a common endeavor? Or are these various practices only superficially related by their being individual spiritual exercises? The latter, apparently, is the point of view of those who have chosen to equate meditation with only a certain type of practice, ignoring all the others that do not fit their description or definition. It is thus that in the Christian tradition meditation is most often understood as a dwelling upon certain *ideas*, or engaging in a directed intellectual course of activity; while some of those who are more familiar with Eastern methods of meditation equate the matter with a dwelling on anything *but* ideas, and with the attainment of an aconceptual state of mind that excludes intellectual activity. Richard of St. Victor, the influential theorist of meditation of the Christian Middle Ages, drew a distinction between meditation and contemplation according to purposefulness and the part played by reason:

Meditation with great mental industry plods along the steep and laborious road keeping the end in view. Contemplation on a free wing circles around with great nimbleness wherever the impulse takes it. . . . Meditation investigates, contemplation wonders.[1]

Other authors distinguish concentration from meditation, regarding the former as a mere drill for the latter. An interesting case of restriction of the term appears in Kapleau's *The Three Pillars of Zen*.[2] He insists that Za-Zen is not to be confused with meditation. This is a paradoxical proposition, since the very word *zen*, from the Chinese *ch'an*, ultimately derives from the concept of dhyana, meditation. Zen Buddhism is, therefore, meditation Buddhism in a real and practical sense. Yet the distinction is understandable in view of the apparent diversity of forms that meditation has taken, even within Buddhism.

The distinction between ideational versus non-ideational is only one of the many contrasting interpretations of the practices called meditation. Thus, while certain techniques (like those in the Tibetan Tantra) emphasize mental images, others discourage paying attention to any imagery; some involve sense organs and use visual forms (mandalas) or music, and others emphasize a complete withdrawal from the senses; some call for complete inaction, and others involve action (mantra), gestures (mudra), walking, or other activities. Again, some forms of meditation require the summoning up of specific feeling states, while others encourage an indifference beyond the identification with any particular illusion.

The very diversity of practices given the name of "meditation" by the followers of this or that particular approach is an invitation to search for the answer of what meditation is *beyond its forms*. And if we are not content just to trace the boundaries of a particular group of related techniques, but instead search for a unity within the diversity, we may indeed recognize such a unity in an *attitude*. We may find that, *regardless of the medium* in which meditation is carried out—whether images, physical experiences,

verbal utterances, etc.—the task of the meditator is essentially
the same, as if the many forms of practice were nothing more
than different occasions for the same basic exercise.

If we take this step beyond a behavioral definition of meditation
in terms of a *procedure*, external or even internal, we may be
able to see that meditation cannot be equated with thinking or
non-thinking, with sitting still or dancing, with withdrawing
from the senses or waking up the senses: meditation is concerned
with the development of a *presence*, a modality of being, which
may be expressed or developed in whatever situation the individual may be involved.

This presence or mode of being transforms whatever it touches.
If its medium is movement, it will turn into dance; if stillness,
into living sculpture; if thinking, into the higher reaches of intuition; if sensing, into a merging with the miracle of being; if
feeling, into love; if singing, into sacred utterance; if speaking,
into prayer or poetry; if doing the things of ordinary life, into a
ritual in the name of God or a celebration of existence. Just as
the spirit of our times is technique-oriented in its dealings with
the external world, it is technique-oriented in its approach to psychological or spiritual reality. Yet, while numerous schools pro-
pound this or that method as a solution of human problems, we
know that it is not merely the method but *the way in which it is
employed* that determines its effectiveness, whether in psychotherapy, art, or education. The application of techniques or tools
in an interpersonal situation depends upon an almost intangible
"human factor" in the teacher, guide, or psychotherapist. When
the case is that of the intrapersonal method of meditation, the
human factor beyond the method becomes even more elusive.
Still, as with other techniques, it is the *how* that counts more than
the *what*. The question of the right attitude on the part of the
meditator is the hardest for meditation teachers to transmit, and
though it is the object of most supervision, may be apprehended
only through practice.

It might be said that the attitude, or "inner posture," of the meditator is both his path and his goal. For the subtle, invisible *how* is not merely a *how to meditate* but a *how to be*, which in meditation is exercised in a simplified situation. And precisely because of its elusive quality beyond the domain of an instrumentality that may be described, the attitude that is the heart of meditation is generally sought after in the most simple external or "technical" situations: in stillness, silence, monotony, "just sitting." Just as we do not see the stars in daylight, but only in the absence of the sun, we may never taste the subtle essence of meditation in the daylight of ordinary activity in all its complexity. That essence may be revealed when we have suspended everything else but *us*, our presence, our attitude, beyond any activity or the lack of it. Whatever the outer situation, the inner task is simplified, so that nothing remains to do but gaze at a candle, listen to the hum in our own ears, or "do nothing." We may then discover that there are innumerable ways of gazing, listening, doing nothing; or, conversely, innumerable ways of *not* just gazing, not just listening, not just sitting. Against the background of the simplicity required by the exercise, we may become aware of ourselves and all that we bring to the situation, and we may begin to grasp experientially the question of attitude.

While practice in most activities implies the development of habits and the establishment of conditioning, the practice of meditation can be better understood as quite the opposite: a persistent effort to detect and become free from all conditioning, compulsive functioning of mind and body, habitual emotional responses that may contaminate the utterly simple situation required by the participant. This is why it may be said that the attitude of the meditator is both his path and his goal: the unconditioned state is the freedom of attainment and also the target of every single effort. What the meditator realizes in his practice is to a large extent how he is failing to meditate properly, and by becoming aware of his failings he gains understanding and the ability to let go of his wrong way. The right way, the desired attitude, is what remains when we have, so to say, stepped out of the way.

If meditation is above all the pursuit of a certain state of mind, the practice of a certain attitude toward experience that transcends the qualities of this or that particular experience, a mental process rather than a mental content, let us then attempt to say what cannot be said, and speak of what this common core of meditation is.

A trait that all types of meditation have in common, even at the procedural level, gives us a clue to the attitude we are trying to describe: all meditation is a *dwelling upon* something.

While in most of one's daily life the mind flits from one subject or thought to another, and the body moves from one posture to another, meditation practices generally involve an effort to stop this merry-go-round of mental or other activity and to set our attention upon a single object, sensation, utterance, issue, mental state, or activity.

"Yoga," says Patanjali in his second aphorism, "is the inhibition of the modifications of the mind." As you may gather from this statement, the importance of dwelling upon something is not so much in the *something* but in the *dwelling upon*. It is this concentrated attitude that is being cultivated, and, with it, attention itself. Though all meditation leads to a stilling of the mind as described by Patanjali, it does not always consist in a voluntary attempt to stop all thinking or other mental activity. As an alternative, the very interruptions to meditation may be taken as a temporary meditation object, by dwelling upon them. There is, for example, a Theravadan practice that consists in watching the rising and falling of the abdomen during the breathing cycle. While acknowledging these movements, the meditator also acknowledges anything else that may enter his field of consciousness, whether sensations, emotions, or thoughts. He does it by mentally naming three times that of which he has become aware ("noise, noise, noise," "itching, itching, itching") and returning to the rising and falling. As one meditation instructor put it: "There is no disturbance because any disturbance can be taken as a meditation object. Anger, worry, anxiety, fear, etc., when appearing should not be suppressed but should be accepted and acknowledged with awareness and comprehension. This meditation is for dwelling in clarity of consciousness and full awareness."

The practice described above is a compromise of freedom and constraint in the direction of attention, in that the meditator periodically returns to the "fixation point" of visual awareness of his respiratory movements. If we should take one further step toward freedom from a pre-established structure, we would have a form of meditation in which the task would be merely to be aware of the contents of consciousness at the moment. Though this openness to the present might appear to be the opposite of the concentrated type of attention required by gazing at a candle flame, it is not so. Even the flame as an object of concentration is an ever-changing object that requires, because of its very changeability, that the meditator be in touch with it moment after moment, in sustained openness to the present. But closer still is a comparison between the observation of the stream of consciousness and concentration on music. In the latter instance, we can clearly recognize that a focusing of attention is not only compatible with, but indispensable to, a full grasp of the inflections of sound.

Our normal state of mind is one that might be compared to an inattentive exposure to music. The mind is active, but only intermittently are we aware of the present. A real awakening to the unfolding of our psychic activity requires an effort of attention greater and not lesser than that demanded by attending to a fixed "object" like an image, verbal repetition, or a region of the body. In fact, it is because attention to the spontaneous flow of psychological events is so difficult that concentrative meditation *sensu stricto* is necessary either as an alternative or a preliminary.

Attending to one's breath, for instance, by counting and remaining undistracted by the sensations caused by the air in one's nose, is a much more "tangible" object of consciousness than feeling-states and thoughts, and by persisting we may discover the difference between true awareness and the fragmentary awareness that we ordinarily take to be complete. After acquiring a taste of "concentrated state" in this situation and some insight into the difficulties that it entails, we may be more prepared for the observation of "inner states."

Such a "taste" can be regarded as a foretaste, or, rather, a diluted form of the taste the knowledge of which might be the end result of meditation. In the terminology of Yoga, that ultimate state is called *samadhi*, and it is regarded as the natural development of *dhyana*, the meditative state, itself the result of an enhancement or development of *dharana*, concentration. Dharana, in turn, is regarded as a step following *pranayama*, the technique of breathing control particular to Yoga, which entails just such a concentrative effort as the spontaneous breathing of Buddhist meditation.

The process leading from simple concentration to the goal of meditation (*samadhi*, *kensho*, or whatever we may want to call it) is thus one of progressive refinement. By practicing attention we understand better and better what attention is; by concentrating or condensing the taste of meditation known to us we come closer and closer to its essence. Through this process of enhancing that *attitude* which is the gist of the practice, we enter states of mind that we may regard as unusual and, at the same time, as the very ground or core of what we consider our ordinary experience. We would have no such "ordinary" experience without awareness, for instance, but the intensification of awareness leads us to a perspective as unfamiliar as that of the world which intensified scientific knowledge reveals to us—a world without any of the properties evident to our senses, materiality itself included.

Awareness, though, is only a facet of that meditative state into whose nature we are inquiring. Or, at least, it is only a facet if we understand the term as we usually do. The meditator who sets out to sharpen his awareness of awareness soon realizes that awareness is inseparable from other aspects of experience for which we have altogether different words, and so intertwined with them that it could be regarded as only conceptually independent from them.

Let us take the classical triad *sat-chit-ananda* according to the formulations of *Vedanta*, for instance. On the basis of the experiential realizations in which we are interested here, these three are our true nature and that of everything else, and the three are inseparable aspects of a unity: *sat* means being; *chit*, consciousness of mind; *ananda*, bliss.

From our ordinary point of view, these three seem quite distinct: we can conceive of being without bliss or awareness, of awareness without bliss. From the point of view of what to us is an unusual or "altered" state of consciousness, on the other hand, the individual sees his very identity in another light, so that he *is* consciousness. His very being is his act of awareness, and this act of awareness is not bliss-ful but consists *in* bliss. While we ordinarily speak of pleasure as a reaction in *us* to *things*, the meditator in samadhi experiences no distinction between himself, the world, and the quality of his experience because he *is* his experience, and experience is of the nature of bliss. From his point of view, the ordinary state of consciousness is one of not truly experiencing, of not being in contact with the world or self, and, to that extent, not only deprived of bliss but comparable to a non-being.

Special states of consciousness are not more expressible than states of consciousness in general, and are bound to the same limitation that we can only understand what we have already experienced. Since the goal of meditation is precisely something beyond the bounds of our customary experience, anything that we might understand would probably be something that it is not, and an attachment to the understanding could only prevent our progress. This is why many traditions have discouraged descriptions, avoided images or positive formulations of man's perfected state or of the deity, and stressed either practice or *negative* formulations:

> It is named Invisible, Infinite, and Unbounded, in such terms as may indicate not what It is, but what It is not: for this, in my judgment, is more in accord with its nature, since, as the capital mysteries and the priestly traditions suggested, we are right in saying that It is not in the likeness of any created thing, and we cannot comprehend Its super-essential, invisible, and ineffable infinity. If, therefore, the negations in the descriptions of the divine are true, and the affirmations are inconsistent with It. . . .
>
> —Dionysius the Areopagite

> The teacher (Gautama) has taught that a "becoming" and a "non-becoming" are destroyed; therefore it obtains that: *nirvana is neither an existent thing nor an unexistent thing.*"
>
> —Nagarjuna

> Never, never teach virtue . . . you will walk in danger, beware! beware!
> Every man knows how useful it is to be useful.
> No one seems to know how useful it is to be useless.
>
> —Chuang-Tzu

Yet positive formulations of what existence looks or feels like in peak states of consciousness abound. When these are conceptual (as in terms of sat-chit-ananda or other trinities), they constitute the experiential core of theologies, theistic or non-theistic. When symbolic, they constitute true religious art, and some great art that we do not conventionally consider "religious." Both types of expression are important to consider in any attempt like ours, which is not properly one of "expressing" but of determining the psychological characteristics of the meditational state. Moreover, the symbols of the meditative state are part of the practice of meditation itself in some of its forms, and we could not bypass their significance in any account of such disciplines.

Though, theoretically, any meditation object could suffice and be equivalent to any other, particular objects of meditation serve (especially for one not far advanced in the practice) the double function of a target of attention and a reminder of that right attitude which is both the path and the goal of meditation.

Just as our experience shows that certain poems, musical works, or paintings can hold our interest without being exhausted while others soon enter the category of the obvious, typical meditation objects partake of the quality of becoming more rather than less after repeated contemplations. A Buddhist sutra or a Christian litany, the symbol of the cross or the Star of David, the rose or the lotus, have not persisted as objects of meditation on the basis of tradition alone but on the grounds of a special virtue, a built-in appropriateness and richness, which meditators have discovered again and again throughout the centuries. Being symbols created by a higher state of consciousness, they evoke their source and always lead the meditator beyond his ordinary state of mind, a beyondness that is the meditator's deepest self, and the presence of which is the very heart of meditation.

We must not forget, however, that symbols, meditation objects, or "seeds" *(bija)* for meditation are only a technique. In contrast to the *directive* approach to meditation, in which the individual places himself under the influence of a symbol, we find a *non-directive* approach in which the person lets himself be guided by the promptings of his own deeper nature. Instead of letting a symbol shape his experience, he attends to his experience as given to his awareness, and by persisting in the attempt he finds that his perceptions undergo a progressive refinement. Instead of holding on to a rigid form handed down by tradition, he dwells upon the form that springs from his own spontaneity, until he may eventually find that in his own soul lies hidden the source of all traditions.

Still another alternative to the guiding influence of the symbol may be found in a purely negative approach, which is directive too, but only in a restrictive sense: instead of taking an object to dwell upon and identify with, the meditator here puts his effort in *moving away* from all objects, in *not* identifying with anything that he perceives. By departing from the known he thus allows for the unknown, by excluding the irrelevant he opens himself up to the relevant, and by dis-identifying from his current self concept, he may go into the aconceptual awakening of his true nature.

The three types of meditation may be represented as the three points of a triangle (as in Figure 1). At one end of the base (line)

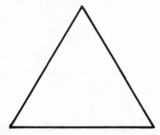

The Negative Way: elimination, detachment, emptiness, centered, the "middle way"

The Way of Forms: concentration, absorption, union, outer-directed, Apollonian

The Expressive Way: freedom, transparence, surrender, inner-directed, Dionysian

Figure 1

is represented meditation upon externally given symbolic objects, and at the other end is the contrasting alternative of meditation upon spontaneously arising contents of the mind. In the former, the person confronts an *other* (idea of God, etc.) upon which he concentrates, in which he sees his own center, with which he identifies, and to which he seems receptive. In the latter, the meditator seeks to become receptive to, and to identify, with *himself*, without the mirror device of the symbol.

In the former approach the individual attempts to interiorize an externally given form, or projects his experience onto it, until his subjectivity is absorbed by the object. In the latter, the individual seeks attunement to an inner form or a formless depth out of which a personal form emerges—in imagery, thoughts, gestures, feelings, or, above all, as an attitude toward the situation at the moment. The former is an assimilative, introjective, or projective process. The latter, a process of expression. One is a formal approach that involves relinquishing of spontaneity, insofar as it keeps the meditator on the path worked by the symbol. The other approach not only does not involve extrinsically given forms, but could be seen as a pursuit of formlessness: the meditator seeks to relinquish expectations, preconceptions, predetermined courses of action, so as to make himself receptive to the promptings of his unprogramed spontaneity. Just as the former is of a hieratic style, the latter is orgiastic; the former entails obedience to a pattern, the latter, freedom from the known; the former is Apollonian, the latter Dionysian.

Different as these two may seem, they converge upon a common end state, for, after all, the forms and symbols that the traditions of mankind offer as starting points for meditation have originated in spontaneity. And, conversely, a surrender to spontaneity leads not to chaos but to the expression of a definite structure that all men share. As Jung showed in the domain of visual fantasy, the images become more "collective"—and therefore similar to the universal patterns of myth—the more the subject explores his presumably individual depth.

In contrast with these two orientations in the task of meditation—one outer-directed and the other inner-directed—the third point in our triangle stands for a purely *negative* approach: not a reaching out or a reaching in but a self-emptying. In this approach the effort is to attain a stillness of the mind's conceptualizing activity, a withdrawal from external perceptions and internal experience alike, to cultivate a detachment toward psychological acting in general. This method is based upon the experiential finding that the state we call wakefulness is in large measure of an inhibiting nature, so that our ordinary mental operations actively preclude or limit the occurrence of states such as those pursued in meditation. If we are able to accomplish nothing more than a stilling of the mind, bringing the goal-directed activity of our ordinary state of consciousness to a standstill, separating temporarily from our ego functions (and still retain consciousness), we may enter an altogether unfamiliar domain of experience without ever having sought it *positively* (*i.e.*, approached it as a goal known through symbolical or conceptual formulations).

2 / Concentrative or Absorptive Meditation

Each of the traditional symbols employed in the different schools of meditation could well be, by itself, the object of an essay larger than the present one. I shall attempt, however, to cast a panoramic glance at some traits shared by the most widespread meditation objects as a means of elucidating the experience elicited by and reflected upon them.

One of the characteristics of the most universal objects of meditation, whether visual, verbal (such as the names of God), acoustical (bell, drum), or other, is what we may call *centrality*. The lotus, the cross, the heart, the sun, a source of light, and many other images more or less explicitly evoke the notion of a center around which actions flow—namely, a center as a point of balance, a source, or an end. Related to the center as a source is the idea of radiation or emanation, also prominent in many of the more widespread meditation objects. Some of these, like white light and fire, are forms of energy and necessarily imply radiation. Others, like the heart, evoke the thought of emanation because of their function as a central mover. Plant symbols, like the lotus, rose, and the seed, express emanation in the aspect of growth; others, like the cross or mandala, express it more directly and geometrically in the pure idea of a center of origin and in vertical and horizontal extension. As to the names of God in different religions, these are also aspects of the ultimate reality, frequently conceived as emanations or extensions of the hidden beyondness of the divine into the field of manifestation. Emanation, be it of goodness, energy, life, consciousness, or existence itself, may also be conceived, in more anthropopsychic terms, as a giving of love. At the same time, though, some symbols convey an understanding of this giving as a self-emptying—such as love or death; the energy and light of the flame being the other side of a sacrifice of that which is burning. Thus the seed must die to become a plant, and the cross, which is the symbol of universal life, is also one of individual surrender and death. In a similar way, only that which makes itself transparent may become full of light, and only that which is empty may be filled. The condition equated with the greatest fullness is also that of nothingness, not in the sense of a nothingness preceding completion, but in that of a void being the ever-present condition, foundation, and ground of fullness. An image that expresses this particularly well is that of the lake of the mind becoming, in its stillness, like a perfect mirror, and in iconography, the invisible or empty center of the mandala and the nothingness at the center of the lotus.

Another aspect of the images that we are considering, not unrelated to those of centrality, radiation, and death-emptiness, is that of order, regularity, and lawfulness. Many symbols convey such lawfulness in their very style, formal and mathematical; others in their inner coherence or allusion to natural processes like growth, radiation, or transformation of energy. The lawfulness of such symbols, simple as an empty circle or complex as a Tibetan mandala, evokes one more aspect of the same single experience that may be viewed as one of giving, of self-emptying, of centering. It is the experience that in theistic formulations is expressed as conformity with God's will and in alternative cognitive maps is expressed as a surrender to a Tao (Way) or Dharma (Law of the Universe).

One particular aspect in which lawfulness is manifested in symbols is in the conciliation of opposites, or, more generally, in the presentation of the unity in multiplicity. Polarity is more explicit in the symbol of the cross, constituted by the intersection of two polarities. It is also explicit in symbols like the Chinese yin-yang and the sacred syllable AUM (the open-mouthed beginning and the close-mouthed ending representing all polarities and dualities). But polarity can also be implicit, as in the symbolism of light, which entails the illumination of a darkness; in that of fire, which must consume something other than itself; or in the mandala-like symbols, which contrast center and periphery, and thus the one and the many.

If we agree that meditation objects are external representations of the "meditation state," and the latter is the meditator's consciousness of himself, we can also say that all object-centered meditation is a dwelling of the individual upon his deepest identity, upon the reflection of himself in the mirror of symbolism. In contrast to this form of meditation, we see in other forms a dwelling upon the self not mediated by symbolism: this is most explicit in Ramana Maharshi's formula of meditating upon the question "Who am I?"[1] and in the "speculation" of medieval platonism. The latter, meaning literally "gazing into a mirror," consisted in concentrating on the pupil of one's own eye, and on one's reflection in it. A reference to this practice is found in the apocryphal Platonic "First Alcibiades," where Socrates relates the Delphic inscription "Know Thyself" to this form of self-contemplation:

> Socrates: but if now the soul wants to know itself, must it not also gaze into the soul, and indeed into its noblest part, that is, where reason and wisdom dwell? This part of the soul resembles the divine. So may it not be that he who turns his gaze thither and learns to recognize everything that is of a divine nature—God and insight by reason—may also, at the same time, learn to know himself with profound recognition?[2]

The centrality of meditation objects is a direct expression of their being a means to our remembrances of the individual's center, the core of his being. In both an inner and an outer sense, they are objects of con-centration. The very word medi-tation refers to a midst or center that we find within us.

Thus, to our former statement that meditation constitutes an exercise of attention, we may add that it is also a practice in centeredness, a practice in being oneself and knowing onself.

But what is this self?

According to the Buddhistic formulation, there is no such thing as "self," and the only image that can convey the experience of attainment is that of sunyata, emptiness. *Sunyata* literally means "no bottom." Just as the center of a mandala is frequently empty, and the center of the cross vanishes into the nothingness of a mathematical point, as the Holy of Holies cannot be entered and the Name of Names cannot be uttered, the core of being is experienced by the meditator's achieving kensho (goal) as bottomless, empty, and endless. It is the night from which proceeds light, the non-being that sustains being, the absence of self at the heart of selfhood.

The "empty" aspect of the meditative state may be seen, at the level of practice, as a direct extension of the concentrative aspect. For concentration intends as exclusion of all activities other than that which medieval mysticism (Jan van Ruysbroeck) calls a mere "staring" and Buddhism calls "bare attention." The actions of "just staring" and "just sitting," and the freedom from thoughts that they intend, represent at the same time a maximization of awareness and the condition of self-abandonment. However, we should not see these two as different phenomena but as inseparable aspects of the whole: awareness *is* receptivity, and "inner silence" must be created before real concentration takes place, a stilling of the mind's lake before it becomes a mirror and can *reflect*. As the Swabian mystic Suso puts it: "If any man cannot grasp this matter, let him be idle and the matter will grasp him."

The culmination of this ego dissolution is achieved in the state called *nirvana* (extinction) in Buddhism and *fana-f'illah* (extinction into God) in Islam. But "extinction" is not another condition but only an *aspect* of the condition to which we have referred as one of awakening (culmination in consciousness) and centering, or identification with the source of one's being. Nirvana is not only the extinction of separateness and illusion but an awakening to reality and the finding of one's identity in the emptiness that contains all things—in themselves impermanent and devoid of self.

The foregoing description of the meditation state as one of awareness-centeredness-emptiness may convey the idea of a condition of feelinglessness, which again would be no more than a half-truth. It is peace (*hesychias*) that the Fathers of the Desert regarded as the landmark of success in their discipline, and equanimity (*upekkha*, sometimes wrongly translated as "indifference") that is the goal of Buddhistic meditation. But, we may ask, do such peace and equanimity signify a lack of feeling or an absence of any reactions toward other beings?

The radiating quality of meditation symbols answers this question in the same way as do the reports from those who have experienced the peak states that we are trying to understand. The enlightened ones are loving and compassionate, and the mystical experience is frequently described as one of deep solidarity with all mankind. Not only the Buddha bears the epithet of "The Compassionate"; in Christianity and Islam, too, love is the most prominent aspect of the godhead, man's highest intuition and experiential realization of the *summum bonum*. "In the name of Allah, the Compassionate, the Merciful . . ." is the formula introducing each chapter of the Koran.

Are equanimity and love, emptiness and compassion, really contradictory? Any close consideration of the matter will show us that, on the contrary, just as in the symbols that depict a growth from an empty center, or in the Tibetan vajra—which is at the

same time emptiness, the hardest stone, and a glittering jewel—
there is a condition in which equanimity may be seen as the
foundation of love, peace as the source of caring, selflessness as the
basis for empathy.

In other words, what occurs when the individual relinquishes
what he is doing is not inaction but a transpersonal process, which
we may see as a much greater action. When he achieves detachment from pleasure and pain, he is not indifferent but free to
live and die, and to enjoy the gift of life without caring about
gain and loss. If this may sound too abstract, the following
anecdote from one of the great Zen masters may show the expression of this state in real life.

> The Zen master Hakuin was praised by his neighbors as one living
> a pure life.
>
> A beautiful Japanese girl whose parents owned a food store lived
> near him. Suddenly, without any warning, her parents discovered
> she was with child.
>
> This made her parents angry. She would not confess who the man
> was, but after much harassment at last she named Hakuin.
>
> In great anger the parents went to the master. "Is that so?" was
> all he would say.
>
> After the child was born it was brought to Hakuin. By this time
> he had lost his reputation, which did not trouble him, but he took
> very good care of the child. He obtained milk from his neighbors
> and everything else the little one needed.
>
> A year later the girl-mother could stand it no longer. She told
> her parents the truth—that the real father of the child was a young
> man who worked in the fish market.
>
> The mother and father of the girl at once went to Hakuin to ask
> his forgiveness, to apologize at length, and to get the child back
> again.
>
> Hakuin was willing. In yielding the child, all he said was: "Is
> that so?"[8]

True indifference is not indifferent. When the individual is
able to remove his little ego (moral ideas included) from the

course of his deeper nature, the melody played by the gods through his hollow reed is one of goodness and beauty:

> Yu replied: I understand. *The music of earth sings through a thousand holes. The music of man is made on flutes and instruments. What makes the music of heaven?*
> Master Ki said: *Something is blowing on a thousand different holes. Some power stands behind all this and makes the sound die down. What is that power?*

—Chuang[4]

> The man in whom Tao acts without impediment
> Harms no other being by his actions.
> Yet he does not know himself
> To be "kind," to be "gentle."

—Chuang[5]

What the Chinese describe as a gentle standing out of the way of the "great blower," or an emptying of the mind, is probably what the more egocentric personality of Western man sees as the violent death of the ego, a self-sacrifice that is the portal to a higher consciousness.

The subject of a conjunction between the experience of love and the acceptance of death is a rich one both at the mythological level and at that of psychological processes. We might say that all love, in that it is a giving of one's self, rests upon a measure of non-attachment, and all life is a consuming of itself.

Perhaps the most significant idea belonging to this domain of love-death is that of sacrifice. We could say that the visible sacrifices that constitute acts of worship in different religions are, like meditation objects, the sacrificer's projections of that state of mind whose aspects are love and self-emptying. "Sacrifice" derives from *sacer facere*, "to make holy," and as usage makes clear, the holy action is one of giving up in pain that is joy. Beyond masochistic distortions of the sacrificial attitude or the understanding thereof, we may see in sacrifice a convergence of the issues of equanimity (transcendence of attachment to pleasure and pain), giving, and death: the giving up of that which is given. The joy of the sacrificer is not a perverse pleasure in pain. If his mind is truly involved in his action, the bliss of the meditation state is a joy *beyond* pleasure and pain, a sense of attunement with the holy that follows upon surrender of personal preference:

> Feelings of heat and cold, pleasure and pain, are caused by the contacts of the senses with their objects. They come and they go, never lasting long. You must accept them.
>
> A serene spirit accepts pleasure and pain with an even mind, and is unmoved by either.
>
> —From the *Bhagavad-Gita*[6]

The detachment from desires encouraged by the Scriptures goes beyond detachment from pleasure and pain and applies to mental formulations of virtue and vice as well. The conventionally virtuous man is no more liberated or open to his true self than the one that is prey to the automatisms of desire. A Hindu saying goes: "A nightingale in a golden cage is no freer than one in a cage of iron." And the Bhagavad-Gita: "The world is imprisoned in its own activity, except when actions are performed as worship of God. Therefore you must perform every action sacramentally, and be free from all attachments to results."[7]

Much of what has been said in the foregoing pages already anticipates that aspect of meditation which is parallel to the lawfulness, regularity, or order of meditation symbols. Non-action that is supreme action, surrender that becomes an attunement to God's will, emptiness that is radiant, death that is eternal life—all these expressions involve the notion of a very *precise* unfolding of experience to which the individual opens himself as he lays aside his habitual patterns of thinking and feeling and his superficial identity. Whereas, from one point of view, his attitudes and experiences may be seen as those of love, from another point of view it is not *his* love, there not being any "self" to do the loving, but only a channel, a field of space where the unfolding can occur. In this sense, the individual can be said to be attuned to a law greater than himself.

> Yet, as a wheel moves smoothly, free from jars,
> *My will and my desire were turned by love,**
> the love that moves the sun and the other stars.
>
> —Dante[8]

We have briefly looked at meditation as a practice in awareness, intensiveness, self-abasement, love, and in attunement to a regularity, which we may choose to regard as God's law or as the law of our own being. We can also see in meditation the development of that characteristic which we mentioned last among those shared by meditation objects: the coincidence of opposites, and, more generally, unity in multiplicity.

Unity and the solution of conflict as a characteristic of mystical experience is something accepted enough so that we need not discuss it here. What is relevant, though, is to show how the expression of unity relates to the others discussed so far, and constitutes only another way of expressing the single experience that is in itself a unity and a silent center in the midst of our many descriptions.

Let us start by considering an aspect of meditation that we have not emphasized and in which the transcendence of duality is most relevant: the disappearance of the habitual distinction between subject and object.

Just as meditation on an object entails concentration on it, it also entails identification with it. The Zen student *becomes* the *koan*, the worshiper is united with his God, the one meditating on the tradition of enlightenment becomes (to the extent that he succeeds in his meditation) the "enlightened one."

From the conceptual point of view, we look at "attending to"

---

* The italics are the author's.

and "identifying with" as two fully different processes. But are they so in actual experience? Complete concentration, complete giving of our attention to something, reaches a point where we are, so to say, pure receptivity filled by the object: not a screen or a mind where the object is reflected, not an "I" that perceives, but a nothingness filled by the contemplation; only the object exists, empathetically perceived, as it were, from within. This need not be an experience arrived at through meditation. More appropriately, we might say that meditation aims at the restoration of the *natural* mode of perception that our conceptual distinctions (like that of subject versus object) have blurred. The following excerpt from the work of a contemporary British author illustrates a spontaneous recovery of that lost naïveté which phenomenology sometimes seeks in vain to recover:

> This book is an unconventional attempt to discover, for myself and in my own way, what I am and what I amount to in the universe.
>
> What am I? That is *the* question. Let me try to answer it as honestly and simply as I can, forgetting the ready-made answers.
>
> Common sense tells me that I am a man very similar to other men (adding that I am five-feet-ten, fortyish, gray-headed, around eleven stone, and so on), and that I know just what it is like here and now to be me, writing on this sheet of paper.
>
> So far, surely, nothing can have gone wrong. But has my common sense really described what it is like to be me? Others cannot help me here: only I am in a position to say what I am. At once I make a startling discovery: common sense could not be more wrong to suppose that I resemble other men. I have no head! Here are my hands, arms, parts of my trunk and shoulders—and, mounted (so to say) on the shoulders, not a head but these words and this paper and this desk, the wall of the room, the window, the gray sky beyond. . . . My head has gone, and in its place is a world. And all my life long I had imagined myself to be built according to the ordinary human and animal plan!
>
> Where other creatures carry small rounded body-terminals, fairly

constant in shape and furnished with such things as eyes and hair and mouth, there is for me a boundless and infinitely varied universe. It looks as if I alone have a body which fades out so that almost the only hints which remain of it above my shoulders are two transparent shadows thrown across everything. (I may call them nose-shadows if I please, but they are not in the least like noses.)

And certainly I do not find myself living inside an eight-inch ball and peering out through its portholes. I am not shut up in the gloomy interior of any object, and least of all in a small, tightly-packed sphere, somehow managing to live my life there in its interstices. I am at large in the world. I can discover no watcher here, and over there something watched, no peep-hole out into the world, no window-pane, no frontier. I do not detect a universe: it lies wide open to me. These ink-marks are now forming on this sheet of paper. They are present. At this moment there is nothing else but this blue and white pattern, and not even a screen here (where I imagined I had a head) upon which the pattern is projected. My head, eyes, brain—all the instruments that I thought were here at the center—all are a fiction. It is incredible that I ever believed in them.[9]

The experience of selfless identification with an object or being is known to all of us in some measure, for it underlies all genuine aesthetic experience, human empathy, and the religious attitude. When we say to somebody "I understand you," we do not mean to convey that we reason and classify his state of mind from without, but that we know it from within. The very word intuition expresses this: *intus-ire*, "to enter," "to place oneself inside."

Aesthetic experience, like that of human empathy, is disinterested, as philosophers of beauty have remarked. The realm of art is divorced from that of practicality. We can only see the play as a play to the extent that we are not personally involved in its slot, and in general we can be open to the sense of beauty when we are free from concern with the useful. The disinterested or gratuitous quality of aesthetic appreciation may help us to understand that of the experience where unity of subject and object reaches a maximum—the state of absorption aimed at by meditation.

Absorption is all that we have enumerated: a concentrated attention, a self-forgetfulness or self-emptying, a giving oneself completely to the matter or situation at hand, a merging with It. If the "It" of the meditator be himself, the resulting experience will be that of merging with himself, and the dissolution of inner duality; if the "It" be God, the experience will be that expressed by St. Paul as "I do not live but Christ lives in me." The attitude of the meditator toward the world was expressively rendered by a Japanese Zen master when he said that we must live with an empty heart, to let the world fill it. The meditator's attitude in face of God is best expressed in Rumi's well-known passage:

> A certain man once came and knocked on the door of a friend.
> "Who are you, faithful one?" his friend asked.
> "I," he answered.
> "Go away," the friend said. "It is not the proper time. There is no place for such a raw fellow at a table like mine."
> . . . then he returned and once more circled about the house of his companion. Fearful a hundredfold, he gently knocked at the door, anxious lest any unmannerly word should escape his lips.
> His friend called, "Who is that at the door?"
> He answered, "You also are at the door, heart-ravisher!"
> "Now," the friend cried, "since you are I, come in, O I! There is not room in the house for two I's."[10]

The perception of unity that characterizes the depth of the meditation state and has been formulated by mystics of all lands entails more than the merging of I and Thou. It is a recognition of oneness in all things and all beings. In monotheistic formulations, all is the expression of one God; in pantheistic renderings of the experience, all *is* God. In non-theistic mysticism, all is a "substance," a thatness, a beingness transcending its own phenomenal manifestations. The oneness of Reality beyond its forms is beautifully expressed in a Sufi tale about an elephant that is brought to a city of blind men:

> The populace became anxious to see the elephant, and some sightless from among this blind community ran like fools to find it.
>
> As they did not even know the form or shape of the elephant they groped sightlessly, gathering information by touching some part of it.
>
> Each thought that he knew something, because he could feel a part.
>
> When they returned to their fellow-citizens eager groups clustered around them. Each of these was anxious, misguidedly, to learn the truth from those who were themselves astray.
>
> They asked about the form, the shape of the elephant: and listened to all that they were told.
>
> The man whose hand had reached an ear was asked about the elephant's nature. He said: "It is a large, rough thing, wide and broad, like a rug."
>
> And the one who had felt the trunk said: "I have the real facts about it. It is like a straight and hollow pipe, awful and destructive."
>
> The one who had felt its feet and legs said: "It is mighty and firm, like a pillar."
>
> Each had felt one part out of many. Each had perceived it wrongly. No mind knew all: knowledge is not the companion of the blind. All imagined something, something incorrect.[11]

In the language of this parable, it would be through an overcoming of blindness that the men could understand that they were confusing the whole with its parts and the being with its attributes, and thus come to see unity where they now experienced diversity. The contemplative act, too, like the overcoming of blindness, may lead to the discovery of a universal whole of which all things are aspects. The absorption of the meditative state is not only one in which the individual becomes the other, but reaches to the essence of the other, which is the essence of everything.

This takes us directly to another characteristic of the meditation object and of the meditative state, which we have not stressed thus far: the religious quality of both. As stated earlier, that essence of all things which is no-thing, that center from which "all" manifests and derives both meaning and value, that essence which the meditator finds in himself by losing himself, is most frequently formulated as "God" or as a cosmic entity of numinous quality. So long has meditation been associated with religion that we take this connection for granted and have ceased to ask whether it is necessary and intrinsic. If meditation is a practice in awareness, in centeredness and equanimity, in attunement to our nature, in the capacity of giving up ourselves and being available to our perceptions, in receptivity and in freedom from preconceptions necessary to reception—does this mean that it is also an act of worship, a religious act?

I think that this question is particularly appropriate at this time when the United States is starting to turn its attention to meditation with a technique-oriented mind developed throughout previous decades, and when we wonder whether feedback training and the control of alpha waves or other brain functions might not perhaps become a substitute for meditation, thus cutting through all theories and theologies and intentions in the person undergoing the discipline.

In examining this aspect of meditation, let us start once more by considering the symbols and their function in practice.

The most widespread meditation objects are the outward expression of a condition of mind after which the individual strives: the self-realized state, the peak of the human condition, the God-man. Emblematic of this are the image of the sitting Buddha, the Bodhisattvas of countless tankas, and the Christ on the cross. These symbols are "religious" to the extent that the inner conditions that they depict are "religious." That some other meditation objects that we have been considering (the lotus, fire, light, heart, etc.) are also emblematic of this mental state that the meditator seeks to cultivate* may be acceptable enough to one who has read the foregoing pages.

In contrast to the symbols that stand for a condition acknowledged as available to man, or even intrinsic to man, another class of symbols stands in the mind of the meditator for the divine being, or spiritual entities outside himself. These objects of meditation, like the names or attributes of God, or the spirits evoked by the magician or shaman, would ordinarily be regarded as religious in the sense that the attitude toward or belief in them and desire for contact or union with them have come to be the very definition of religion.

A contemporary psychologist, with his knowledge of projection, would naturally lean toward the monistic point of view, in which the many images of God conceived by man are regarded as an externalization of his own experience, or aspects of himself.

On the other hand, because of the gap between man's ordinary condition and the God-state, no model could be more true to man's experience than the dualistic one, in terms of which he sees the divine being outside of and beyond himself. Perhaps it is because of this that even in the non-theistic religions the dualistic point of view has a prominent place in the emotional attitude of the seeker of enlightenment. Even though the Mahayana Buddhist may intellectually assert that the "other shore" is this one, his experience is one of aspiration, the intuition of a reality beyond the limitations of his ego, and the feeling of devotion typical of the religious spirit throughout the world.

Moreover, as Lama Govinda has remarked, "Even the Buddha of the Pali texts did not refrain from calling the practice of the highest spiritual qualities (like love, compassion, sympathy, equanimity) in meditation a "dwelling in God" (*brahmavihara*) or in a "divine state."[12] In this context, the divine is not merely a projection into a beyond of man's object and longing, but a term

* To the extent that we may speak of cultivation, because the meditator *is* what he seeks and he seeks what he is.

needed to speak of an actual experience of attainment, and the question naturally arises as to why the most *human* qualities should be ascribed to an entity beyond man. The reason does not lie, I believe, in the mere contrast between man's best and his ordinary condition, a contrast that leads to considering the former as something extraordinary and as the fulfillment of the natural as unnatural. Aside from this and aside from the aptness of the "divine" to symbolize the highest values, the essence of "otherness" may be found in the very essence of man's obedience to his true nature. Our "virtues" have their source in our very being, and their absence in the betrayal of man's true reality. But this "true self" of ours—unlike our self-assertive ego—is but a channel for the expression of natural laws. To the extent that we are "ourselves," we are also a part of the cosmos, a tide in the ocean of life, a chain in the network of processes that do not either begin or end within the enclosure of our skins. This thought, which anyone can grasp conceptually, appears to have been the experiential realization of men of all lands who, in surrendering to their true being, felt, too, that they were becoming part of an organism greater than themselves. Just as if a cell were to understand itself as a small component of a larger organism, so man's experience of true naturalness is inseparable in his mind from that of being supported by greater laws, and of being a mere branch in the tree of life, an individual embodiment of the Way (Tao, the Law; Dharma, God's will). The images of this "greater whole" vary according to their individual interpreters as much as the different parts of the elephant in the Sufi tale. But all, from the nature mystic to the worshiper of a God-outside-the-world, imply the experience of self-as-part, self-as-vehicle or instrument, self-as-field-of-expression-for-the-whole, self-as-channel—which is to say that the experience of self-reality goes hand in hand with the individual's experience of selflessness or emptiness as discussed earlier.

In the Buddhistic outlook, the "self" has been an illusion all along, a conceptual separation of the individual from the matrix of being. According to others, like the Islamic, the ego is pictured as a reality that must die. Yet these are but semantic differences, alternative ways of symbolization. All mysticism acknowledges the underlying experience of self-emptying and a merging with the unity of being. Compare, for instance, the following documents:

1. In Attar's *Parliament of Birds*, when the thirty survivors among the questing birds, after crossing the seven valleys, find the Simurgh, the king whom they were seeking, "the sun of majesty sent forth his rays, and in the reflection of each other's faces these thirty birds (Si-Murgh) of the outer world contemplated the face of the symbol of the inner world. This so astonished them that they did not know if they were still themselves or if they had become the Simurgh. At last, in the state of contemplation, they realized that they were the Simurgh and that the Simurgh was the thirty birds. When they gazed at the Simurgh, they saw that it was truly the Simurgh that was there, and when they turned their eyes toward themselves they saw that they themselves were the Simurgh. In perceiving both at once, themselves and Him, they realized that they and the Simurgh were the same being. No one in the world has ever heard of anything to equal it." And some lines later the Simurgh says, "Annihilate yourselves, then, joyfully and gloriously in Me, and in Me you shall find yourselves."[13]

2. "In archery," said Mumeji, Japanese Master of Archery, "a man must die to his purer nature, the one which is free from all artificiality and deliberation, if he is to reach perfect enjoyment of Tao. Learn how to control the emittance of truth, flowing like an eternal spring . . . this way is a very easy and direct one. The most difficult one is to let oneself die completely in the very act of shooting. To facilitate the death of the lower self, a man must exercise unceasingly to gradually acquire the right attitude."[14]

3. And Richard of St. Victor: "The soul which is plunged in the fire of divine love is like an iron, which at first loses its blackness and then growing to white heat, it becomes like the fire itself. And lastly, it grows liquid, and losing its nature is transmuted into an utterly different quality of being."[15]

The interdependence between the experience of self-emptying and the surrender to God, Tao, Dharma, or Reality can be the basis for understanding the connection between meditation proper and the practices men regard as ritual, cult, or prayer. Meditation emphasizes the cultivation of receptivity, of emptiness; worship (including prayer) emphasizes the establishment of a connection between an ego-imprisoned consciousness and a reality beyond its boundaries. He who prays stands before an "other," and in fact prayer has been defined as "standing in the presence of God." Such a connection, which is the goal of devotionalism, requires, to become effective, a measure of ego loss, which is also the goal of meditation. Conversely, the achievement of receptivity in the meditator implies that the individual becomes transparent toward reality. In the forms of meditation involving an object, visual or imaginary, it is to the reality symbolized therein that the individual makes himself open, thus coming close to the attitude of the worshiper. In forms that do not involve a dwelling upon a divine being, or upon symbols of the ultimate reality or of the self, the individual dwells upon his experience, surrenders to his own existence, becomes receptive to *what is* without the focusing lens of a symbolic construction. Meditation and worship can only artificially be divorced; effectiveness in either leads to the discovery of the other, and most forms of practice contain elements of both. If this is not always obvious, it is because of the unfortunate fate of rituals, which usually become "mere rituals" and of the tendency of objects of worship to become divorced from their true function as instruments of a spiritual exercise, to the point of ending up as mere objects of superstition. By regarding meditation objects as symbols for the meditator's goal—

symbols that are to him the reminders of what he is, symbols that he *becomes* in a process that is at the same time self-emptying and self-expression—we have become aware of several aspects of that subtle action which is meditation beyond its apparent form of external procedure. We have looked at meditation as an exercise in centering, both in the sense of concentration of our energies and in that of finding the center of our being. We have looked at it as an exercise in surrender to our true nature, in receptivity, in naturalness, and in allowing a flow of energies normally buried under our roles, our self-programming, our conscious intentions and preconceptions. We have looked at meditation as an act of unification, both in the sense of transcending the duality of subject and object and in that of standing in equanimity beyond the polarities of our personality. We have seen an element of worship in meditation and noticed that "worship" is only another way of speaking of that single experience of devoted attention to receptive apperception of a being or thing which becomes to us an expression of our own highest values.

In discussing meditation objects up to this point, we have spoken mostly of visual images and ideas, which does not do justice to the whole domain of concentrative meditation. The process of giving one's entire attention to a mental image and identifying with it, for instance, is not qualitatively different from the physical enactment of such an image, and in this way we can understand the use of mudra, postures and gestures evocative of certain inner conditions. And just as an image itself need not be static but may include movement, the physical enactment of images (in the process of which the meditator suppresses his identification with his "object") may take the form of physical movement. Some types of meditation-in-movement have remained such, like dervish and some kinds of Tibetan dancing. Other types, like Tai Chi Chuan, are frequently approached by persons seeking goals (health, self-defense) other than the original ones. Still others, like Indonesian dancing, have evolved into art forms, in which the aim of entertainment has been developed to the point where the original purpose of the discipline has been forgotten.

The connection between meditation and the arts is by no means limited to the field of classical dance and drama, where the interpreter lends his physical being to an archetypal form, but extends to all domains of artistic creation. In the case of classical Indian sculpture, for example, the artist was supposed to engage in a complex series of inner actions requiring long practice before working with his materials in the outer world:

> The artist (*sadhaka*, *mantrin*, or *yogin*, as he is variously and significantly called), after ceremonial purification, is to proceed to a solitary place. There he is to perform the "Sevenfold Office," beginning with the invocation of the hosts of Buddhas and Bodhisattvas, and the offering to them of real or imaginary flowers. Then he must realize in thought the four (infinite) modes of friendliness, compassion, sympathy, and impartiality. Then he must meditate upon the emptiness (*sunyata*) or non-existence of all things, for, "by the fire of the idea of the abyss, it is said, there are destroyed beyond recovery five factors" or ego-consciousness. Then only should he invoke the desired divinity by the utterance of the appropriate seed-word (*bija*) and should identify himself completely with the divinity to be represented. Then finally, on pronouncing the *dhyana mantra*, in which the attributes are defined, the divinity appears visibly, "like a reflection" or "as in a dream," and this brilliant image is the artist's model.[16]

Not only is the process of deliberate identification with an archetype the bridge between meditation and worship and between meditation and art, but it is also at the basis of magical evocation. Compare, for instance, the following quotation with the previous one from Buddhist sources:

> Let us describe the magical method of identification. The symbolic form of the god is first studied with as much love as an artist would bestow upon a model, so that a perfectly clear and unshakeable mental picture of the god is present to the mind. Similarly,

the attributes of the god are enshrined in speech, and such speeches are committed perfectly to memory. The invocation will then begin with a prayer to the god, commemorating his physical attributes, always with profound understanding of their real meaning. In the second part of the invocation, the voice of the god is heard, and His characteristic utterance is recited.

In the third portion of the invocation, the magician asserts the identity of himself with the god. In the fourth portion, the god is again invoked, but as if by Himself, as if it were the utterance of the will of the god that He should manifest in the magician.[17]

Just as art forms that originated as spiritual disciplines have become divorced from their original intention, much of "magic" can be seen as an empty shell or superstitious mystification of a discipline not different from the one we are concerned with.

To the extent that psychiatry today is assimilating part of what was the function of traditional spiritual disciplines, psychotherapy, too, is incorporating techniques of meditation—deliberately or not. Some psychotherapists have become interested in traditional forms of meditation (Fromm[18] and Heider[19]); others have investigated the psychotherapeutic effectiveness of meditation techniques (Deikman)[20] or have introduced these in their practice. Others have originated psychotherapeutic methods based upon principles similar to meditation, sometimes without intending to imitate or modify traditional forms.

Two types of psychotherapeutic practice are of particular relevance to the discussion of concentrative or absorptive meditation: the psychotherapeutic use of *acting*, as in role-playing, psychodrama, and Gestalt therapy; and the use of suggestion.

The growing incorporation of dramatic resources into psychotherapy probably stems from a recognition that acting, in virtue of its demanding *empathy* from the actor, may be a royal road to intuitive understanding. In acting we understand something by *becoming* it rather than by thinking *about* it. And to identify is —from a different perspective—to establish contact with and express *pre-existing* feelings or experiences in us that match the enacted object.

There is a notable difference between the newer techniques and the attempt of traditional meditators to identify with their object and thus obtain absorption. This difference lies in the choice of the object, which in the traditional forms is typically archetypal and, more, a symbol of integration. In contemporary psychological practice, on the other hand, the typical object is a personification of an aspect of the individual's personality involved in conflict. These contrasting approaches can be characterized as being "the way of ascent" and the "way of descent": the effort to explore, contact, and assimilate the many fragments of the psyche, which may have to be integrated into the Divine Whole versus the direct attempt to identify with the qualities of wholeness.*

The question of similarities and differences between states of concentrative meditation and hypnotic states is an involved one, and I will not discuss it here in detail. But, as in meditation, concentrated attention upon an object and repetition are the main avenues to hypnosis, and in both states the individual may enter a "trance." Whereas in deep hypnosis the individual is usually amnestic of the episode and, in general, hypnotic trance is best described as a state of *restricted* awareness, meditation does not involve amnesia and awareness is expanded, if anything.

Another similarity between suggestion and meditation with an object is that in both cases the individual *places himself under the influence of symbols*—verbal, visual, or other—and experiences the consequent effects of the symbols on his emotions, his body, or states of mind.[21]

Suggestion, as usually practiced in supportive psychotherapy or hypnotherapy, may be regarded as a form of manipulation in which the psychotherapist evokes the desired states in the mind

* This is discussed more fully later. See pp. 65ff.

of a willing subject. In many of the techniques of psychosynthesis (as in self-hypnosis), we may speak of a self-manipulation
in which the individual employs the knowledge of how symbols
may create feeling states. In general, a meditator is one who has
acquired the ability to control inner states—not in the sense of
filtering-suppressing control, but in that of being able to *create* his
mental states.

This ability of self-manipulation may appear to be an alternative
to genuineness; thus, when we speak of "acting" we tend to interpret the word as mere simulation rather than as a creating of
true feelings. Valid as the distinction between deliberateness and
spontaneity may be in terms of subjective experiences, I believe,
however, that at depth we are *always* acting and that there is a
condition of consciousness where the contradiction between deliberateness and spontaneity disappears. At some level, *all* our
mental states are our choice—but "we" do not identify much
with the doer of our actions. The meditator may reach the point
at which he is one with his deeper self, one with the responsible
agent for whom every experience is a choice, all life a conscious
game. Just as the words "speculation" and "reflection" have
shifted in meaning from the original one of non-conceptual receptivity to that of discursive thinking, so has the term "meditation"
itself. In common parlance, "meditate" has come to mean "think
about." In the course of history we have forgotten that it meant
the art of "dwelling upon" topics and ideas. Yet this *dwelling
upon* an idea, which really constitutes meditation, is the very
opposite of *thinking about*. In the highly anti-intellectual tradition of Zen Buddhism, meditation on thought forms has a prominent place (at least in the Rinzai school) in the form of koan
practice.

A koan is a meditation object that, in spite of being presented
to the medium of thought, still defies any attempt to think about
it. It is a statement that at the same time expresses a state of consciousness and is cryptic to the reasoning mind, so that it can be

apprehended only through intuition. Or, more precisely, it is apprehended by him who shares the understanding from which it sprang. Isshu Miura, in commenting on a verse of Fu-Daishi, quotes: "If, on coming upon expressions such as these, you feel as if you were meeting a close relative face to face at a busy crossroad and recognizing him beyond a question of a doubt, then you can be said to understand the Dharmakaya.* But if you use common sense to conjecture about it, or run hither and thither trying to follow the words of others, you would never know the Dharmakaya."[22]

Zen students are encouraged not to discuss their koan practice among themselves, and, anyhow, such a discussion is regarded as something as intimate and subtle as that of one's way of making love. Without going into the intimacy of the meditative process, it may be of interest to read what D. T. Suzuki has written of his autobiographical experience with the first two koans that he received in his instruction. The following quotation emphasizes the total involvement of the meditator with his task, to the point where it becomes a matter of life or death. This is a point that I have not stressed enough and that might be overlooked in a treatment of meditation as a mere "exercise." Dr. Suzuki tells us how for about a year he worked unsuccessfully on his first koan until his teacher died. The roshi that succeeded changed the earlier koan to *Mu* and then

> There followed for me four years of struggle, a struggle mental, physical, moral, and intellectual. I felt it must be ultimately quite simple to understand *Mu*, but how was I to take hold of this simple thing? It might be in a book, so I read all the books on Zen that I could lay my hands on. The temple where I was living at the time, Butsunichi, had a shrine attached to it, dedicated to Hojo Tokimune, and in a room of that shrine all the books and documents belonging

---

* "The realm which is revealed to us when we see into our true nature," according to one of many definitions. The understanding of the Dharmakaya is the content and objective of many koans.

to the temple were kept. During the summer I spent nearly all my time in that room, reading all the books I could find. My knowledge of Chinese was still limited, so many of the texts I could not understand, but I did my best to find out everything I could about *Mu* intellectually. . . . Then in the way of moral effort I used to spend many nights in a cave at the back of the Shariden building where the Buddha's tooth is enshrined. But there was always a weakness of will power in me, so that often I failed to sit up all night in the cave, finding some excuse to leave, such as the mosquitoes.

I was busy during those four years with various writings, including translating Dr. Carus's *Gospel of Buddha* into Japanese, but all the time the koan was worrying at the back of my mind. It was, without any doubt, my chief preoccupation, and I remember sitting in a field, leaning against a rice stack and thinking that if I could not understand *Mu* life had no meaning for me. . . .

It often happens that some kind of crisis is necessary in one's life to make one put forth all one's strength in solving the koan. This is well illustrated in a story in the book *Keikyoku Soden, Stories of Brambles and Thistles,* compiled by one of Hakuin Zenshi's disciples, telling of various prickly experiences in practising Zen.

"A monk came from Okinawa to study Zen under Suio, one of Hakuin's great disciples and a rough and strong-minded fellow. It was he who taught Hakuin how to paint. The monk stayed with Suio for three years working on the koan of the sound of one hand. Eventually the time for him to go back to Okinawa was fast approaching, and he had still not solved his koan; he got very distressed and came to Suio in tears. The Master consoled him, saying, 'Don't worry. Postpone your departure for another week and go on sitting with all your might.' Seven days passed, but still the koan remained unsolved. Again the monk came to Suio, who counselled him to postpone his departure for yet another week. When that week was up and he still had not solved the koan, the Master said, 'There are many ancient examples of people who have attained satori after three weeks, so try a third week." But the third week passed and still the koan was not solved, so the Master said, 'Now try five more days.' But the five days passed and the monk was no nearer solving the koan, so finally the Master said, 'This time try three more days, and if after three days you still have not solved the koan, then you must die.' Then, for the first time, the monk decided to devote the whole of whatever life was left to him to solving the koan. And after three days he solved it."

The moral of this story is that one must decide to throw absolutely everything one has into the effort. "Man's extremity is God's opportunity." It often happens that just as one reaches the depths of despair and decides to take one's life, then and there satori comes. I imagine that with many people satori may have come when it was just too late. They were already on their way to death. . . .

This crisis or extremity came for me when it was finally settled that I should go to America to help Dr. Carus. . . . That winter might be my last chance to go to sesshin, and if I did not solve my koan then, I might never be able to do so. I put all my spiritual strength into that sesshin.

Until then I had always been conscious that *Mu* was in my mind. But so long as *I* was conscious of *Mu* it meant that I was somehow separated from *Mu*, and that is not a true samadhi. But towards the end of that sesshin, about the fifth day, I ceased to be conscious of *Mu*. I was one with *Mu*, I identified with *Mu*, so that there was no longer the separateness implied by being conscious of *Mu*. This is the real state of samadhi.

But this samadhi alone is not enough. You must come out of that state, be awakened from it, and that awakening is Prajna. That moment of coming out of the samadhi and seeing it for what it is —that is satori.

. . . I would like to stress the importance of becoming conscious of what it is that one has experienced. After kensho I was still not fully conscious of my experience. I was still in a kind of a dream. This greater depth of realization came later while I was in America, when suddenly the Zen phrase . . . "the elbow does not bend outwards" became clear to me. "The elbow does not bend outwards" might seem to express a kind of necessity, but suddenly I saw that this restriction was really freedom, the true freedom, and I felt that the whole question of free will had been solved for me."[23]

The "irrational quality" of the koan has a parallel in the Sufi use of jokes as meditation objects. The humorous effect of jokes is precisely linked to that paradoxical quality in them of a break in logical consistency that is still not a break in coherence at a non-logical level of understanding. There is a whole corpus of literature consisting of stories attributed to the seemingly foolish wise man Nasrudin, many of which have spread throughout the world as jokes to which nobody gives a second thought. Here is a Middle Eastern version of a familiar story, told in the words of Idries Shah:

> On one occasion a neighbor found [Nasrudin] down on his knees looking for something.
> "What have you lost, Mulla?"
> "My key," said Nasrudin.
> After a few minutes of searching, the other man said, "Where did you drop it?"
> "At home."
> "Then why, for heaven's sake, are you looking here?"
> "There is more light here."[24]

Though the story makes enough sense at a first reading to elicit a humorous response, the reader might be interested in exploring its meaning further by devoting a few minutes of exclusive attention to the situation depicted. Furthermore, he might ponder on the possible meaning of losing the *key*, of the statement that it lies at *home*, of *searching* for it where there is more *light*. He may find it useful for this end to enact the story in his mind, and *be* Nasrudin, the key, the home, the light, the friend. Last, he might recapitulate by inquiring to what extent Nasrudin's predicament is his own, "trying it on for size." "*I* am searching for the key in the wrong place," etc. These Nasrudin stories are given much importance in some Sufi orders. "The use to which the tales of Nasrudin are put in Sufi circles," writes an informant, "shows that the intention of the teacher is to develop in the student the form of thinking which is different from customary patterns. . . . Certain levels of human understanding cannot be attained, it is claimed, until the brain can work in more than one way. This is the equivalent of what in some systems is a 'mystical illumination process' but the Naqshbandis seem to hold that the brain is prepared by degrees without this illumination being as violent an experience as in other methods."[25]

When the seed idea constituting the meditation object is one that can be put in a few words, repetition of such words may serve as a means for the meditator to avoid distraction. Just as concentration in breathing is important, among other things, for its being a more concrete act of awareness than that of inner states, so, too, concentration on a verbal repetition lends a tangible support to the object of meditation, and this helps to ensure continuity in awareness.

Repetition of words or phrases may be vocal, subvocal, written, or in the medium of visual imagery. Still, the nature of the practice in each case is beyond the mechanical appearance of its outward form. As in all meditation, the goal of the exercise is the absorption of the individual in the idea upon which he dwells, and no amount of repetition would substitute for the right attitude and perhaps the proper guidance. The following autobiographical passage from Mohammed Alawi is revealing as to the "inner dimensions" of such a practice. Speaking of his teacher, he says:

His way of guiding his disciples, stage by stage, is varied. He would talk to some about the form in which Adam was created and to others about the cardinal virtues, and to others about Divine Actions, each instruction being especially suited for the disciple in question. But the course which he most often followed, and which I also followed, was to enjoin upon the disciple the invocation of the single name with the distinct visualization of its letters until they were written in his imagination. Then he would tell him to spread them out and enlarge them until they filled all the horizon. The dhikr would continue in this form until the letters became like

light. Then the Sheikh would show the way out of this standpoint
—it is impossible to explain in words how he did so—and by means
of this indication the spirit of the disciple would quickly reach
beyond the created universe provided that he had sufficient preparation and aptitude—otherwise there would be need for purification
and other spiritual training. At the above-mentioned indication, the
disciple would find himself able to distinguish between the Absolute
and the relative, and he would see the universe as a bowl or lamp
suspended in a beginningless endless void. Then it would grow
dimmer in his sight as he persevered in the invocation to the ac-
companiment of meditation, until it seemed no longer a definite
object but a mere trace appeared. Then it would become not even
a trace, until at length the disciple was submerged in the World of
the Absolute and his certainty was strengthened by Its Pure Light.
In all this the Sheikh would watch over him, and ask him about his
faith and strengthen him in the dihkr degree by degree until he
finally reached the point of being conscious of what he perceived
through his own power. The Sheikh would not be satisfied until this
point was reached, and he used to quote the words of God which
referred to 'one whom his Lord hath made certain and whose
certainty he hath then followed up on direct evidence.'

When the disciple had reached this degree of independent perception, which was strong or weak according to his capability, the
Sheikh would bring him back again to the world of outer forms
after he had left it, and it would seem to him the inverse of what it
had been before, simply before the light of his inward eye had
dawned. He would see it as *Light Upon Light*, and so it had been
before in reality.[26]

The practice of oral repetition is widespread in the form of
mantras and litanies, in recitation of sutras, in kirtan (chanting
of divine names, in Hinduism), the Nembutsu, in the practice
of Pure Land Buddhism, and in certain forms of prayer. Its highest development is probably to be found in Sufi circles, where
the exercise holds a prominent role and is known as *dhikr*, which
means repetition and also remembrance. This is an apt double

meaning, for the notion of "remembrance" is as appropriate to the psychological aspect of the exercise as "repetition" is to the physical or literal. In the Moslem tradition the utterance of the name of God is related to God's injunctions through the hand of the prophet: "Remember your Lord in yourself with compunction and awe. . . . Remember Me and I will remember you." In these we can see what we have pointed out as an aspect of meditation throughout these pages: meditation is a summoning up within oneself of a state of being that is not something to be created but our deepest reality. For this reality of ours to awaken, on the other hand, "we" must stand aside. This, translated into the complete words of the dhikr, means that the zakir (remembrancer) gives his attention more and more to the meaning of what is said, until he "is not so much busy with the dhikr (remembrance) as with the mazkur (the one invoked or remembered)."[27] This double movement of affirming the transcendent unity of existence and denying the attachments of the ego to partial reflections of the One Truth is the content of one of the most widespread forms of dhikr: the repetition of the words of the Prophet Mahomet: "LA ILAHA ILLA'LLAH" (There is no god but God).

The following passage from *Najmeddin Daya*, a thirteenth-century Sufi classic, is most explicit on both the outer and inner aspects of the repetition:

Having prepared a room which is empty, dark, and clean, in which he will, for preference, burn some sweet-scented incense, let him sit there, cross-legged, facing the qibla (direction of Mekka). Laying his hands on his thighs, let him stir up his heart to wakefulness, keeping a guard on his eyes. Then with profound veneration he should say aloud: LA ILAHA ILLA'LLAH. The LA ILAHA should be fetched from the root of the navel, and the ILLA'LLAH drawn into the heart, so that the powerful effects of the Zikr (dhikr) may make themselves felt in all the limbs and organs. But let him not raise his voice too loud. He should strive, as far as possible, to damp and lower it according to the words 'Invoke thy Lord in thyself humbly and with compunction, without publicity of speech.' . . .

After this fashion, then, he will utter the Zikr frequently and intently, thinking in his heart on the meaning of it and banishing every distraction. When he thinks of LA ILAHA, he should tell himself: I want nothing, seek nothing, love nothing ILLA'LLAH—but God. Thus, with LA ILAHA he denies and excludes all competing objects, and with ILLA'LLAH he affirms and posits the divine Majesty as his sole object loved, sought and aimed at.

In each Zikr his heart should be aware and present (hazir) from start to finish, with denial and affirmation. If he finds in his heart something to which he is attached, let him not regard it but give his attention to the divine Majesty, seeking the grace of help from the holy patronage of his spiritual Father. With the negation LA ILAHA let him wipe out that attachment, uprooting the love of that thing from his heart, and with ILLA'LLAH let him set up in its place the love of Truth (God).[28]

In reading the account above, in which the *content* is emphasized, one might overlook the importance ascribed to the *form* or phonetical aspect of most verbal repetition.

The names of the deity and divine attributes and emanations (just as those of the angels, demons, or djinn invoked by the magican) are highly important in all traditions as a key to the success of the theurgic operation. The particular name of the spiritual force is like a key that may unlock its power, and in this light we may understand the importance attached by Egyptian priests to words uttered under certain conditions (remarked by the distinguished Egyptologist Sir E. A. Wallis Budge) or of the secret pronunciation of the tetragrammaton.*

The thought that words and sounds may have a "power" may be understandable and acceptable to a modern mind if formu-

---

* Israel Regardie mentions a legend according to which "he who knows the correct pronunciation of YHVH, called the Shemha-Mephoresh, the Unpronounceable Name, possesses the means of destroying the universe, his particular universe, and hurling that individual consciousness into samadhi."[29]

lated in terms such as the following: the "powers" invoked by the words are states of consciousness and aspects of our psyche.* In a natural symbolism, there is a relationship between these and specific sounds, as there is between these and specific gestures, postures, colors, parts of the body, and elements of nature. To some extent, this is something that every good poet recognizes and uses implicitly when he chooses the appropriate phonetic expression for his ideas.† A word is a conventional symbol in that a given meaning is arbitrarily ascribed to a given string of sounds. But words are also *natural* symbols in that they their sound structure evokes in us a certain feeling state or an atmosphere of associations. In the first sense, a word is an intellectual symbol; in the second, a feeling symbol—*i.e.*, the bearer of a direct experience.

The use of the purely phonetical and non-intellectual aspect of word symbolism has apparently reached its maximum development in the Hindu tradition of Mantra Yoga and is also an important component of Vajrayana (Tibetan Buddhism). According to the mantra shastra, each element or category of the universe has its own natural sound, which is called its seed (*bija*). Each one of the elements has its mantra, and new mantras arise from the combination of these. Each deity has a mantra, and every mantra a deity. AUM has been called the queen of all mantras, and their source as well. There exists a whole literature on the significance of AUM and the technique of meditation thereon.

The phonetic aspect of a poem may be highly expressive to one who understands its words, so that form then becomes to the

* Francis Barrett, the British forerunner of Eliphas Levi, states in *The Magus:* "All the spirits, and as it were the essences of all things, lie hid in us, and are born and brought forth only by the working, power (will) and fantasy (imagination) of the microcosm."[30]
† Even in the natural structure of languages there seems to be a component of phonetic symbolism not to be explained as mere onomatopoeia. In a study that has become a classic, Roger Brown demonstrated that when English-speaking subjects were presented with pairs of antonyms in English, Chinese, Hindu, and Czech, they were able to match the English to appropriate terms of the other languages unknown to them with a degree of success beyond chance.[31]

content what blood is to the body. On the other hand, the same sounds will be without expressive value to one who does not have an understanding of the language. In a similar fashion, the claim that certain sounds are better than other sounds, expressions, and remembrances of certain experiences does not imply that the effectiveness of mantra is independent of the meditator's knowledge of its significance. In other words, mantras are not expected to be "magical" in the sense of being mechanically effective. Sir John Woodroffe, who devoted much attention to the subject, states quite explicitly: "The utterance of a mantra without knowledge of its meaning, or of the mantra method, is a mere movement of the lips and nothing more. The mantra sleeps. There are various processes preliminary to and involved in its right utterance. . . ."[32]

Mantra, like visual symbols, postures, or ideas, are mere screens for the meditator to project aspects of his goal. The quality of the screen counts, but no meditation object is a real meditation object while it remains a mere object.

If we now return to a consideration of the dhikr described earlier, we will notice that the exercise is more than the repetition of certain words. It is obvious from the description that, like many other forms of meditation (in the broad sense used in this work), the exercise represents a coherent composite of several elements: among others, an attitude of repentance and purity, a feeling of veneration, a quality of awareness or "wakefulness," a selfless humility, love of God, and detachment from all other affections.

Even in an outer sense, this form of dhikr is more than the repetition of a formula, for "the LA ILAHA should be fetched from the root of the navel, and ILLA'LLAH drawn into the heart, so that the powerful effects of the dhikr may make themselves felt in all the limbs and organs." This aspect constitutes a bridge between the mantric aspect of the dhikr (verbal repetition) and still another type of concentrative meditation, which we will discuss here only briefly in spite of (and because of) its particular importance—that in which the meditation objects are certain areas of the body and their related functions or aspects of existence.

Meditation on the body "centers," the chakras of the Hindu and Tibetan systems, and the lataif[33] of the Arabic system, constitutes a complex spiritual science (just as that of the mandala or mantra), but elements of this knowledge are widespread as components of other types of meditation. Just as the dhikr is frequently a composite exercise bringing together into a coherent whole a number of different techniques, so are most forms of meditation. Even the utterly simple practice of counting the breath in the Zen tradition brings together quite a number of technical components: sustained awareness of breathing; spontaneity of the breath function not affected by watchfulness (a form of nondoing); stillness; an enactment of the posture of the sitting Buddha at the moment of enlightenment as a means to evoke the meditator's basic identity or Buddha nature; a posture of the hands (*maha mudra*) signifying the union of opposites, or specifically the identity of samsara and nirvana; the direction of attention to the belly region, so that the body is perceived as *centered* in an area that constitutes its natural center, and so on.

In many of these composite practices the body is given a special importance. Even when it is with images, ideas, or sounds that the meditator is concerned, these are considered to be located within the body, or as related to it, so that it could be said that his body becomes the temple for his ritual.

An example of the above may be found in the "Prayer of the Heart" of the Christian tradition. This prayer, which constituted the basic discipline of the early Fathers of the Church (and was later cultivated particularly by the Hesychast monks of Mount Athos), may well called the Christian dhikr. The following passages from St. Simeon the New Theologian (contained in the *Philokalia**) should make this apparent:

* An ascetic-mystical anthology, compiled in the eighteenth century, probably by Macarius of Corinth and Nicodemus of the Holy Mountain, and first published in Venice in 1782. It contains writings of the Fathers of the Christian Church of the first millennium.

There are three methods of attention in prayer, by which the soul is uplifted and moved forward, or is cast down and destroyed. Whoever employs these methods at the right time and in the right way, moves forward. . . .

Attention should be linked to prayer as inseparably as body is linked to soul. . . . Attention should go on ahead, spying out the enemy, like a scout. . . .

The distinctive features of the first method are as follows: if a man stands in prayer and, raising his hands, his eyes and his mind to heaven, keeps in mind Divine thoughts, imagines celestial blessings, hierarchies of angels and dwellings of the saints, assembles briefly in his mind all that he has learned from the Holy Scriptures and ponders over all of this while at prayer, gazing up at heaven, and thus inciting his soul to longing and love of God, at times even shedding tears and weeping, this will be the first method of attention and prayer.

But if a man chooses only this method of prayer it happens that, little by little, he begins to pride himself in his heart, without realizing it; it seems to him that what he is doing comes from God's grace. . . .

This method contains another danger of going astray; namely, when a man sees light with his bodily eyes, smells sweet scents, hears voices and many other like phenomena. Some have become totally possessed, and in their madness wander from place to place. . . .

The second method is this: a man tears his mind away from all sensed objects and leads it within himself, guarding his senses and collecting his thoughts, so that they cease to wander amid the vanities of this world; now he examines his thoughts, now ponders over the words of the prayer his lips utter, now pulls back his thoughts if, ravished by the devil, they fly toward something bad and vain, now with great labour and self-exertion, strives to come back into himself, after being caught and vanquished by some passion. The distinctive feature of this method is that it takes place in the head, thought fighting against thought. In this struggle against himself, a man can never be at peace in himself, nor find time to practise virtues in order to gain the crown of truth. Such a man is like one fighting his enemies at night in the dark; . . . because he himself remains in the head, whereas evil thoughts are generated in the heart. He does not even see them, for his attention is not in his heart. . . .

Truly the third method is marvelous and difficult to explain. . . . If someone observes perfect obedience towards his spiritual father, he becomes free from all cares, because once and for all he has laid all his cares on the shoulders of his spiritual father. Therefore, being far from all worldly attachments, he becomes capable of zealous and diligent practice of the third method of prayer, pro-vided he has found a true spiritual father, who is not subject to prelest. . . .

The beginning of this third method is not gazing upward to heaven, raising one's hands, or keeping one's mind on heavenly things; these, as we have said, are the attributes of the first method, and are not far removed from prelest. Neither does it consist in guarding the senses with the mind and directing all one's attention upon this, not watching for the onslaughts of the demons on the soul from within. . . .

Proceeding in this way you will smoothe for yourself a true and straight path to the third method of attention and prayer which is the following: the mind should be in the heart—a distinctive feature of the third method of prayer. It should guard the heart while it prays, revolve, remaining always within, and thence, from the depths of the heart, offer up prayers to God. (Everything is in this; work in this way until you are given to taste the Lord.)

. . . As to other results which usually come from this work, with God's help, you will learn them from your own experience, by keeping your mind attentive and in your heart holding Jesus, that is, His prayer—Lord Jesus Christ, have mercy upon me! One of the holy fathers says: 'Sit in your cell and this prayer will teach you everything.'[34]

The same source offers other descriptions and indications as to breathing, aside from those of the repetitive prayer and the attention directed to the heart area. The following is a passage from the Patriarch Callisotis and his fellow-worker Ignatius of Xanthopoulos:

"You know, brother, how do we breathe: we breathe the air in and out. On this is based the life of the body, and on this depends its warmth. So, sitting down in your cell, collect your mind, lead it into the path of the breath, along which the air enters in, constrain it to enter the heart together with the inhaled air, and keep it there. Keep it there, but do not leave it silent and idle; instead give it the following prayer: 'Lord, Jesus Christ, Son of God, have mercy upon me.' Let this be its constant occupation, never to be abandoned. For this work, by keeping the mind free from dreaming, renders it unassailable to suggestions of the enemy and leads it to Divine desire and love."[35]

One particular element of Nadi Yoga, which frequently occurs in association with apparently dissimilar practices, is its first stage: that of centering, or focusing attention, in the lower abdomen.* This region is called in Japanese *hara*, a word that signifies not only the center of the body but also the center of the soul, and is a prominent concept in the culture of that country. According to Durkheim:

There are master schools that make *hara* the sole object of their exercise, while every master art in Japan considers that it is necessary to possess it in order to achieve "success" in whatever one is doing. To a Japanese, what a man experiences in the "center of being" is none other than the unity of life, bearing all, permeating all, nourishing and enfolding all.[36]

When we deal with spiritual disciplines that involve the manipulation of images or sounds, we can conceive these as "symbolic" and say that the symbol evokes a psychological reality, or that the individual in his meditative absorption "becomes" what the symbol represents. When we deal with the domain of anatomical objects of meditation, can we consider these as merely symbolic? Is, for instance, a condition of physical cen-

---

* Some methods emphasize the solar plexus (as in the position of hands in Za-Zen), while others choose a point under the navel, and others the "root chakra."

teredness in the abdominal area a mere symbolic expression of a psychological or spiritual centeredness, or is the psychophysical parallelism the expression of the fact that each single condition of being is mirrored in the domain of both psyche and soma?

If we think that we *are* our body, we will have no trouble understanding the powers of the body-centered techniques of meditation in affecting the individual's state. If, on the other hand, we prefer to regard physical localizations as symbolic of inner states, we cannot fail to see that this is a symbolism more natural and "closer to home" than any other. In this symbolism, our whole body stands for our "self" (as we ordinarily imply when we say, for instance, "Don't touch me!") and different regions of the body relate to different domains of experience.*

In the Tantric tradition of India and Tibet, the body is seen as a field of a double polarity: one, the right-left (*ida* and *pingala*, "sun" and "moon"; *ha-tha*, involution-evolution); and the other, above-below (consciousness and power, spirit and matter). The spiritual work consists in the unification of these opposites and the attainment of the center of a symbolic cross. The integration of this double polarity "is experienced in successive stages, namely in successive chakras, of which each represents a different dimension of consciousness, and in which the higher dimension includes the lower one without annihilating its qualities."[38]

More precisely, the body is regarded as comprising in the vertical plane three regions: head, chest, and abdomen, and in each of these are located the chakras that express particular specializations of the character of each region. The systems of Hindu and Buddhistic Tantras here diverge. The former speaks of three chakras in each of the extreme regions, which, added to the heart chakra, give a total of seven. The Buddhistic tradition,

* The work of Sheldon might be taken as an indication that this is more than symbolism.[37]

on the other hand, takes into account only two chakras each in the head and in the abdominal region, and thus deals with a system of five.*

The chakras are regarded as positive and negative (and, in the Hindu Tantras, neutral) particularizations of the functions expressed by the three regions of the body. This type of body symbolism is quite natural, and one that is implicit in our current speech when we say that a person "has guts" or "is kind-hearted," or that somebody "lives in his head." Here is a brief characterization of the lower, upper, and middle regions in the words of the Lama Angarika Govinda:

> Lower: A terrestrial plane, namely that of earth-bound elementary forces of nature, of materiality, corporality, an emphasis on the "materialized past";
>
> Upper: The cosmic or universal plane of eternal laws, of time-less knowledge (which from the human point of view is felt as a "future" state of attainment, a goal yet to be attained), a place of continuous spiritual awareness of the Infinite, as symbolized in the boundlessness of space and in the experience of the Great Void (*sunyata*) in which form and non-form are equally comprised;
>
> Middle: The human plane or individual realization, in which the qualities of terrestrial existence and cosmic relationships, the forces of the earth and of the universe, become conscious in the human soul as an ever-present and *deeply felt* reality. Therefore, the Heart Center becomes the seat of the seed-syllable HUM in contradistinction to the OM of the Crown Center.[39]

The formulations of the Taoist system of meditation are quite similar. There are in man three currents or rivers (called "seed," "breath," and "spirit"), which are in correspondence, but not identical, with their physical manifestations and in turn are influenced by them. These three "humors," which might be rendered as a force of generation, a vital force, and a spiritual

* Vajrayana Buddhism eliminates the *swadhist chakra* (the gential center) and its upper correspondent, *ajna chakra* (between the eyebrows).

force, must be united to generate the immortal man, the "diamond body." In accordance with this conception, "There are three points of departure for meditation . . . , namely the 'three fields of cinnabar' . . . or fields of the alchemical elixir: the 'upper' field is in the middle of the forehead, seat of the 'radiance of our essential nature' . . . ; the 'middle' field is in the heart, the true source of the cinnabar-red elixir and of the conscious soul . . . ; and the 'true' field is in the middle of the body (approximately from the navel to the kidneys) seat of the vital force . . . and of the lower soul. . . ."[40]

For the sake of clarity, we have been dealing separately with different areas of symbolization in which the meditator may dwell, different sense-modalities in which he may find the reflection of his "object." But here it may be appropriate to note that the most elaborate meditation systems take advantage of the correspondence between different domains. This might seem to contradict one of the characteristics of meditation indicated earlier: that of one-pointedness of attention or concentration. We can understand how this is not really so if we make a distinction between the perceptual basis of the meditation object, which may be called the *apparent object*, and the experiential meaning conveyed by it, which constitutes the *object itself*. Only at the latter level of meaning can the meditator achieve identification with his "object." In fact the "object" has been himself all along, so that what he does in the process of such unification is to *re-absorb* the meaning projected into the image, sound, or other symbol, and experience it fully as himself.

When we consider the case of meditation techniques involving a single sensory object—visual, motoric, musical, mantric, somatic—concentration on the evoked meaning coincides with concentration on the percept, and we may speak of "concentration" in the usual technical sense. When we consider multi-media meditation, though, concentration on the meaning upon which the different symbolic media converge is paralleled by the division of attention among the images, sounds, actions, etc., that may be involved in that particular sadhana. Yet that apparent division of attention is only superficial: the simultaneous meditation objects that a person contemplates (*i.e.*, bija, mantra, and chakra) are *in essence* the same (if not complementary aspects to be united in a more encompassing whole).

Though some of the practices described in the foregoing pages are, as we have remarked, composites that bring together a number of technical devices, a further example may give a fuller picture of the systematic use of a multisymbolic approach to meditation. This is a Tibetan practice, whose object is the generation of the "inner fire" and in which one may see the superimposition of devotionalism, meditation on the breath, contemplation of images, Chakra Yoga, and mantra:

After the Sadhaka [artist] has purified his mind through devotional exercises and has put himself into a state of inner preparedness and receptivity; after he has regulated the rhythm of his breath, filled it with consciousness and spiritualized it through mantric work, he directs his attention to the Navel Centre (*Manipura*), in whose lotus he visualizes the seed-syllable RAM and above it the seed-syllable MA, from which latter emerges *Dorje Naljorma* (Sanskrit: *Vajra-Yogini*), a *Khadoma* of a brilliant red colour surrounded by a halo of flames.

As soon as the meditator has become one with the divine form of the *Khadoma* and knows himself as *Dorje Naljorma*, he places the seed-syllable A into the lowest, the seed-syllable HAM into the highest, Centre (the "thousand-petalled Lotus" of the Crown Centre).

Thereupon he arouses, by deep conscious respiration and intense mental concentration, the seed-syllable A to a state of incandescence; and this, being fanned and intensified with every inhalation, grows steadily from the size of a fiery pearl to that of a fierce flame, which through the middle *nadi* finally reaches the Crown Centre from where now the white nectar, the Elixir of Life, issues from the seed-syllable HAM (which the meditator has placed and visualized in this Centre) and while flowering down, penetrates the whole body.

This exercise can be described in ten stages: in the first the *susumna*, with its rising flame, is visualized as fine as a hair, in the second stage as thick as a little finger, in the third of the thickness of an arm, in the fourth as light as the whole body, *i.e.*, as if the body itself had turned into a *susumna* and had become a single vessel of fire. In the fifth stage, the unfolding vision attains its climax; the body ceases to exist for the meditator. The whole world becomes a fiery *susumna*, an infinite, raging ocean of fire.

With the sixth stage begins the reverse process of integration and perfection; the storm abates and the fiery ocean is re-absorbed by the body. In the seventh stage the *susumna* shrinks to the thickness of an arm; in the eighth to the thickness of a small finger; in the ninth to that of a hair; and in the tenth it disappears altogether and dissolves into the Great Void (Sanskrit: *sunyata*) in which the duality of the knower and the known is transcended and the great synthesis of spiritual completeness is realized.[41]

At this point we may draw a distinction between two types of meditation objects according to the domain of perception to which they belong. On the one hand, there are those that we examined first and found to express centrality, radiation, emptiness, etc., and that may be taken to express the totality of man's being or essential nature (the cross, OM, fire, etc.). On the other hand, there are meditation objects that are more restricted in meaning, standing for more particular aspects of man's psyche (the crescent, the syllable AH, water).

Most mantra, chakras, and images correspond to *specific* facets of man's appearance, which will eventually become the object of unification with complementary aspects through a meditative process like the one quoted above, or through a ritual operation. In terms of these strategies we may distinguish contrasting systems of meditation. In one, the individual evokes the ultimate goal, the center of his being, the object of his highest aspiration, and most exalted state. In the other, his goal appears to be less ambitious, for he is evoking only a part of his being, and for that very reason his operation is more likely to succeed. The ultimate goal, though, even in this approach, is the bringing together into an encompassing totality of all the faculties or experiences first meditated upon one after another.

In the Tibetan exercise of gtum-mo, for instance, the end result is expressed in the symbol of integration: "The fire of spiritual integration which fuses all polarities, all mutually exclusive elements arising from the separateness of individualization, this is what the Tibetan word *gtum-mo* means in the deepest sense, and what makes it one of the most important symbols of meditation."[42] The approach here is different from that of Vedic ritual, where absorption in the sacrificial fire is both the end and the beginning. In the Tibetan practice described by Govinda, the fire is the result of the polarity and union of two opposite principles, symbolized in A and HAM. A is the seed-syllable of the female or mother principle, and HA that of the male or father principle. A is wisdom (*prajna*) and HA love; the final M, written in Tibetan as a dot (*bindu*), symbolizes the union. Moreover, the symbolic action of unification is expressed in one more aspect of the sadhana under discussion:

"... the seed-syllable A which represents the principle of cognition in the above-mentioned meditative practice, and which the Hinduistic chakra system characteristically associates with the Centre of inner vision (ajna chakra), is to be visualized in the lower centre, namely at the entrance of *susumna* (the Root Centre is here not to be contemplated), while the seed-syllable HAM, here representing the creative principle or Elixir of Life, is visualized in the Crown Centre. This visualization is a symbolic anticipation of the aim, as may be seen from the fact that only when the heat of the flaming A reaches the HAM, the latter is activated and liquefied ... into the degenerative force of an enlightened consciousness which fills the thousand-petalled lotus and, overflowing from it, descends into all the other centres.[43]

Systems like the one above, and Tantras on the whole, might appear as unwarrantedly complicated when contrasted with the simplicity of the Christian mystic's way to *ekstasis* or the practice of *shikan-taza* in Zen Buddhism. But such complexity is merely another expression of the understanding that simplicity is not as simple to achieve as it might seem. To invoke the highest goal requires a knowledge of the goal. To dwell upon the deity requires an experience of the sacred. To "see into one's nature" requires a previous breakthrough into reality.

There is in classical Buddhism a meditation exercise called the "recollection of nirvana" or the "recollection of peace," in which the meditator should in solitude and seclusion "recall the qualities of nirvana," which is defined as the appeasing of all ill, with the words: "As far as there are dharmas, conditioned or unconditioned, dispassion has been thought as the highest of these dharmas, *i.e.*, the sobering of thought-intoxication, the removal of thirst, the uprooting of clinging, the halting of the round (of samsara), the extinction of craving, dispassion, stopping, Nirvana (Anguttara Nikaya, 1134). Like the other five 'recollections,' though, the text informs us that this one *"can be properly and successfully accomplished only on the level of sainthood."*44 This parallels the statement of alchemists that in order to make gold, one must have gold.

In addition to this type of meditation, which has the potential of leading into full trance, Buddhistic scriptures of the same school describe many others that are conceived as preliminaries, their aim being less distant. It is illustrative to consider the list presented by the fifth-century Buddhaghosa in his "Path of Purity" ("Visuddhimagga"):

Ten Devices: 1. earth; 2. water; 3. fire; 4. air; 5. blue; 6. yellow; 7. red; 8. white; 9. light; 10. enclosed space.

Ten Repulsive Things: 11. swollen corpse; 12. blueish corpse; 13. festering corpse; 14. fissured corpse; 15. gnawed corpse; 16. scattered corpse; 17. hacked and scattered corpse; 18. bloody corpse; 19. worm-eaten corpse; 20. skeleton.

Ten Recollections: 21. the Buddha; 22. the Dharma; 23. the Samgha; 24. Morality; 25. Liberality; 26. Devas; 27. Death; 28. What belongs to the body; 29. Respiration; 30. Peace.

Four Stations of Brahma: 31. Friendliness; 32. Compassion; 33. Sympathetic joy; 34. Even-mindedness.

Four Formless States: 35. Station of endless space; 36. Station of unlimited consciousness; 37. Station of nothing whatsoever; 38. Station of neither perception nor non-perception.

One Perception: 39. of the disgusting aspects of food.

One Analysis: 40. into the four elements.[45]

According to Edward Conze:

Two only among the forty are always and under all circumstances beneficial—the development of friendliness and the recollection of death. The remainder are suitable only for some people, and under quite definite circumstances. The recollection of Buddha, for instance, demands strong faith, and even-mindedness presupposes great proficiency in the "Stations of Brahma" which precede it. In this way, some of the meditations may be outside a person's range, others may meet with insuperable resistance, others again may fulfill no useful purpose. Because, as such, the exercises have no value in themselves. They are only cultivated as antidotes to specific unwholesome and undesirable states.[46]

We find a similar situation if we turn to classical yoga. In his twenty-first sutra, Patanjali says: "It [samadhi] is closest to those who desire it intensely." And in the twenty-third, he adds that samadhi can also be attained by self-surrender to God (*isvara-pranidhana*). This is a statement that has puzzled commentators, for Shamkya philosophy, in terms of which Patanjali's Yoga is formulated, is atheistic. On the other hand, it is not upon surrender to isvara that Patanjali lays emphasis as a means of enlightenment, but on the techniques of Astanga Yoga, which is based upon the development of concentration and will. Still, he cannot bypass the existence of that universal experience, which is the heart of the devotional path. Mircea Eliade answers his own question as to Patanjali's need to introduce isvara by saying that isvara corresponds to an experimental fact; in fact, isvara may provoke samadhi if only the yogi practices the exercise called isvara-pranidhana, that is to say, if he takes isvara as the goal of his actions. In attempting to bring together and classify all the valid techniques of yoga in the "classical tradition," Patanjali could not dismiss unusual experiences only obtained through concentration on isvara. That is: aside from the traditions of an exclusively "magical" Yoga which only appeals to will and the personal resources of the ascetic, there was another tradition, a "mystical" one, in which the last stages of Yoga practice were facilitated, at least, by means of a devotion . . . toward a God.[47]

Just as the "mystical" tradition (in the restricted sense) reaches upward in affirmation, the "magical," which we might better call "technical" or perhaps "theurgic," stresses a deepening in the contemplation of our present level of experience, or even a furrowing into an underworld upon which our experience is based. This reaching downward is no doubt the source of the "devilish" associations to the Tantric and magical traditions, as well as the source of some real dangers. This way of descent, immortalized by Dante in his journey through hell, is that of establishing contact with the repressed and suppressed, with those "dormant powers" without which no unity of being would be possible.

A medieval medallion with the text of the famed Emerald Tablet of Hermes Trismegistus bears an inscription that expresses in condensed form the leading idea of the journey of descent. It is an acrostic on the word "vitriol," the Latin for the corrosive sulphuric acid: *Visita Interiora Terrae Rectificando Invenies Occultum Lapidem.* (Visit the inside of the earth. In rectifying you will arrive at the secret stone.) The philosopher's stone, which is the goal of the alchemistic pursuit and which has the virtue of turning "baser metals" into "gold," is to be found through a "corrosive" action upon the earthy side of existence rather than by aspiring toward the lofty heights.

The expressions of this movement of descent in the spiritual disciplines of mankind have been various. One aspect of it is what Dante's hell obviously represents: a journey of self-exploration. Here contemplation is not directed to symbolic embodiments of the spiritual goal nor to particular aspects of the psyche, but toward experience unmediated by symbols. A serene, impartial observation of what we are, not limited to or biased by what we judge as "good," cannot help leading to a re-evaluation of what we are, and eventually to a "seeing into our true nature." The second embodiment of the strategy of descent is in the use of symbolic forms to awaken the inhabitants of our dark underworld from their slumber. Professor Tucci writes:

> The ancient phantoms, the memory of a primitive and far-off world, the monsters and strange figures of primeval gods, the fruits of barbarous and cruel intuitions live on in the depths of our souls and it would be vain to attempt their suppression. They would re-appear unexpectedly on the edge of our subconscious. Gnosis does not deny them, does not drive them back, but *guides* them, as guests of the senses, toward more noble paths, or *transforms* them.

The point of view on which this operation is based is an optimistic one that sees all the undesirable drives in the human personality as a mere imbalance or misapplication of natural forces that are not evil in themselves. The archetypal images used to personify and summon up the forces, therefore, are images that serve as models that direct them to their proper channels. In general, the symbolism of dark deities that mankind has created may be seen in this light. When the Greek genius conceived Dionysus as a mad god, it was seeing godliness even in human madness, and bowing in trust to the forces of chaos within the individual soul. Only today are we beginning to think that this may be after all the most satisfactory way of dealing with and "curing" psychosis.* When the Hindus conceived of Shiva, the destroyer, they were acknowledging the destructive aspect of

* See pp. 106ff.

any creative action, and the positive—even indispensable—role of aggression in life. It can be expected that meditation on Shiva would lead the individual to the assimilation of his insight and to his finding a constructive course for his own aggressive potential. The "dark" figures of Dionysus, Persephone, and others, the idea of descent to a netherworld and the process of psychological "death" prior to renewal, were dominant in the Mysteries of antiquity, and it is small wonder that these pagan rites (or what remained of them through the European Middle Ages) came to be seen by Christian eyes as satanic masses and cults of the devil. European Christianity, with its asceticism, was an attempt to reach God by transcending nature; the Mystery religions, quite the opposite, found the universal soul-spirit *in* nature and attempted a synthesis in which natural man would be included and exalted.

A third aspect of the way of descent in meditation is the importance given to the body. The upward-reaching West, with its pointed cathedral spikes and its Faustian striving, has apparently wanted a short-cut to heaven, and in spite of Jesus' statement that the kingdom of heaven is within, this has mostly been envisaged as above the body. Accordingly, whenever physical techniques were employed in Christian mysticism, they met some criticism and did not become part of the main historical tradition.* By contrast, the East has always given great importance to psychophysiological techniques as a means of enlightenment.

The East in general has asserted what only the esoteric tradition has maintained in the West: that man, and specifically the body, is a microcosm reflecting the macrocosm. In the body dwell all the gods, but they must be awakened. Or, in the language of the Alexandrian Gnostics, the body is the cross to which our Christ-nature is nailed, the tomb in which our spirit lays imprisoned.

* We find, for instance, comments by Church authorities to the effect that the breathing exercises of the Hesychasts were something of the devil.

There is a passage in the Surangama Sutra where Buddha ties one knot after another in a handkerchief, and after each he asks his disciple Ananda, "What is this?" After having tied the seventh knot and heard an identical answer from Ananda, Buddha explains that not all knots are the same because of the order in which they have been tied. "If we wish to untie a knot, we must first find out how the knot was tied. He who knows the origin of all things, knows also their dissolution. But let me ask you another question: Can all the knots be untied at the same time?

"No, Blessed Lord! Since the knots were tied one after another in a certain order, we cannot untie them, unless we follow the reverse order."

To start with the last knot, in the Buddhist darshan, means to start with the body, and within the body (in the chakra system) with its most bodylike region, the foundation, or lower area. The contrast between East and West in this last aspect is also suggestive of the predominant spirit of the respective cultures: Western man, in his ambition to fly out of his body, has identified with the head or, at lowest, with the heart. Orientals, with no less spiritual ambition, have stressed the importance of attaining rootedness in the body first and have cultivated the feeling of the center of gravity in the belly. This experience, which might appear to be a matter of trivial psychological gymnastics, has proved to be an exercise of far-reaching consequences. As may be seen from the following description by Professor Rousselle, the pursuit of centeredness on the abdominal region is the dominant element in the method of Taoistic meditation:

1. Choose a quiet room, neither dark nor bright. In a bright room, one is disturbed by outward images, in a dark room, by inner images.

2. Choose a comfortable position, which the body will not be compelled to change soon, a sitting position. Crossing of the legs in the traditional tailor's posture is quite unnecessary for anyone not

accustomed to it. On the contrary, it is a good idea to set the feet firmly on the ground.

3. Hold the back straight (supported by a back rest if desired) and the head high but bent backward a little, so that the tip of the nose is vertically over the navel and the "light of the eyes" can easily be directed toward the body's center (solar plexus), *i.e.*, so that consciousness can easily be directed toward the unconscious.

4. Keep the eyes half closed. The same would be true of entirely open or entirely closed eyes as of bright or dark rooms. The eyes —their gaze converging over the tip of the nose—are directed toward the solar plexus.

5. Hold the hands together, as in the Chinese greeting—the right hand forms a fist which is held clasped by the left. This represents a *communio naturarum* of the yin and yang.

6. Before beginning to meditate, breathe from three to five times, deeply, slowly and evenly, so that the "sea of breath" (*ch'i hai*) is stimulated in the abdomen. In this way you will avoid being disturbed in the course of meditation by the need to take a deep breath. During meditation, pay no attention to breathing. The mouth must be closed, you must breathe entirely through your nose.

7. Look reverently at the picture of the Master (in the student's certificate). Thus you will be in his presence as it were, and will keep yourself open to meditation with confidence.

8. Banish all thought. A total emptiness of mind is created. Meditation consists in "letting go." It is not the surface consciousness but the creative genius of the deep psyche that should speak to us.

9. This emptiness of thought is facilitated by its positive counterpart, which consists in directing consciousness toward the body's center, *i.e.*, the unconscious.

10. You now enter upon the first of the three preparatory stages of meditation. All thoughts are bound fast in imagination to the body's center (*eros!*) like monkeys at the foot of a tree. The bond between *logos* and *eros* paralyzes the "monkey" thoughts. Consciousness by an act of the imagination is shifted to the solar plexus, i.e., the unconscious. This fixation is called *ting* (c.f., in Indian Yoga, dharana).

11. This produces a certain degree of relaxation, though there is still a faint striving to hold fast. This second preparatory stage of release or silence is called *ching*.

12. One now attains the third stage, in which there is no further effort or tension, the state of peaceful beatitude (*an*).

Now at last the stage has been reached in which something can "happen" to you. What you now experience is the content of your meditation—but images and ideas must be expelled at once! It is impossible to guess beforehand what this content will be. Certain temporary disturbances of the meditation will occur, but these are actually an indication that you have meditated correctly.[48]

It would be artificial to separate completely the two approaches that we are outlining, one of ascent and the other of descent; one of contemplating unity and the other of exploring multiplicity; one, a knocking at the door of the heart of things, and the other a starting at the periphery. There are systems like the meditation on the sephira in European Cabala, or the meditation on mandalas, in which these two movements are like in-breath and out-breath. The mandala, for instance, is a "cosmogram" or "psychogram" to which the meditator journeys with the mind from the multiplicity of the fourfold periphery to the center, and from the center again into the periphery, thus bringing about his own unification and relating from his center to the multiplicity of light.

Still, the predominance of one or another approach in some methods justifies raising the question of their comparative merit. May any one be said to be more appropriate than the other, in general, or are the "mystical" and "technical" ways appropriate to different kinds of men? Opinions as to the unparalleled merit of this or that particular system of meditation are easy to find in any school, and the great number of discordant statements may be a reason to doubt their impartiality. Devotional mystics, for instance, tend to regard the whole idea of technique as foreign to the spiritual domain, and frequently conceive the higher states of consciousness as gifts of grace that may not be earned. "The grace of contemplation," says Bernard of Clairvaux, "was granted only in response to longing, and importunate desire." And even this desire is a gift of divine grace; it is not man who seeks God but God who seeks man. The prayer of Christian mystics is *oratio infusa*, imparted, inspired from above.

But even if the illumination of grace be God's gift, can we make ourselves receptive to it? Empirical research is still to be carried out to ascertain whether the gifts received by a Christian devotionalist or by a Sufi, a Pure Land Buddhist, or a yogi are comparable.

Aside from the possibility of one or another type of meditation being more effective in general, or more appropriate to a certain type of individual, there is the possibility that the ways of descent and ascent may be suited to different stages of spiritual unfolding. One of the most memorable expressions of this is to be found in the *Divine Comedy*. Dante describes how, soon after waking up halfway along the course of his life and finding himself in a dark forest, lost, he saw the rays of the sun illuminating the summit of a mountain.

> Then I looked up, and saw the morning's rays
> Mantle its shoulder from that planet bright
> Which guides men's feet aright on all their ways.[49]

When he proceeded, full of hope, to walk toward the higher goal, however, he found that the enterprise was impossible. His way was obstructed by three successive animals, so terrifying that he realized that he had to give up the attempt of climbing. At this point, in his despair, Virgil appeared to him to guide him, but Dante's journey would now be *un altro viaggio: another* journey. The short way to the "Mount Delectable from which grows the beginning of all joy" being barred, he would have to take that long detour through the Kingdom of the Dead: he would have to *descend* before being able to *ascend* (the Mountain of Purgatory). In his version of the spiritual quest, the descent into hell is the very means of overcoming the obstacles to his ascent: for each of the animals blocking the way, there will be a corresponding region or level in the underworld. The journey through hell is thus analytical and introspective: it is one of confrontation with the passions, the moving forces of one's life in their chaotic actuality. It is an enterprise of pure awareness. The ascent of Mount Purgatory, by contrast, is an act of striving and of devotion in which the soul is lifted by remembrance of its goal.

Is this the path of only one individual, Dante Alighieri, or is there a truth in it that applies to the human condition in general? Should we think of the journeys into multiplicity and into unity, into the given and into the possible, into the soul and into God, as successive states rather than as parallel ways? If so, the way for a given individual would depend upon his station along the path.

Another contrast to be seen among the forms of object meditation described thus far (not unrelated to what has just been discussed) is that between techniques that involve varying degrees of support in the physical world. Thus, at one end of the gamut, we find exercises like concentration on a single mental image. Close to the other end, there are practices like the Tibetan meditation, mentioned above, that involve simultaneous use of breathing, visualization, mantra, and chakra Yoga. Yet, here the images are still internalized, the sound silent, the chakras used merely as aids to the location of visual images. Much richer in sensory experience is the practice of the European occultist who, wanting to invoke Hermes, stands within an octagon surrounded by inscriptions peculiarly relevant to Hermes' nature, in an environment where color predominates and where burns the incense storax.

In commenting precisely on this ceremony, Israel Regardie draws attention to the contrast that we are examining, which he equates with that between mysticism and magic:

Mysticism ordinarily conceives of the senses as barriers to the light of the soul, and that the presence of the latter is debarred from manifestation by reason of the disruptive influence and turbulence of the senses and mind. In magic, however, the senses are considered to be, when under control, the golden gateways through which the King of Glory may come in. In the work of invocation, every sense and each faculty must be made to participate.[50]

On the other hand, as we have commented in regard to mantra, a ritual can be psychologically effective only if the actions and perceptions that it involves are saturated with meaning. Then we may ask: if the meaning is what counts, why complicate meditation with unnecessary images, actions, sounds, or paraphernalia? There is an Oriental tale that brings the point home.

A conventionally minded dervish, walking along the shore of a lake, heard another dervish give the dervish call incorrectly uttered. Considering it a duty to correct the unfortunate person who was mispronouncing the syllables, for this was probably someone who had had no guidance and was probably "doing his best to attune himself to the idea behind the sound," he hired a boat and traveled to the island from where the loud shout came. He corrected the other dervish, who thanked him, and felt satisfied with his own good deed. After all, it is said that a man who could repeat sacred formulas correctly could even walk on the waves.

While he was thinking like this, he suddenly saw a strange sight. From the island the other dervish was coming toward him, walking on the surface of the water. "Brother," he said to him when he was close enough, "I am sorry to trouble you but I have come out again to ask you the standard method of making the repetition you were telling me, because I find it difficult to remember it."[51]

If the essence of meditation is in an attitude, why so many rituals and techniques? The answer can be the same as to why employ symbolic forms in general. Why books, if what counts is meaning and not the words? Why music, if what counts is feeling and not the sound?

The ideal of meditation should be such a firm grasp on the "meaning" that forms become unnecessary,* such a direct contact of the person with reality that he needs no technique. What is the use of the scaffold once the house has been built?

Symbols serve to indicate something beyond themselves, but symbols can also become veils, usurping the place of that which they symbolize. Religious and artistic forms, philosophical *Weltanschauungen*, all stem from certain experiences or from the elicitation of experiences. Yet most religious and artistic images and philosophical forms have become petrified symbols, mere icons that do not speak any more.

Aware of the propensity of individuals to become attached to dead husks and substitute the word expressing the image for the spirit behind it, some mystical traditions have emphasized forms of meditations that bypass symbols, rituals, and ideas. In these, the attitude is all important, and the object may be anything or nothing.

True, in doing away with objects and procedures we do away with the danger of mistaking the issue and taking the outer trappings for the real aim. But how can this all-important attitude be communicated? It is easy to write at length about this or that *technique* of meditation, but how are we to describe a meditation without technique? This becomes as difficult as painting the smile of the Cheshire cat without the cat.

The simpler the meditation object becomes, the less prone the meditator is to fall in love with any counterfeit substitute of his heart's desire, and the more he is on his own in the search, unsupported by a language of forms. Christian mystics speak

* In his essay on contemplation in Christian mysticism, Heiler states: "Contemplation is directed toward the ultimate, the highest, the absolute, toward God in His totality and infinity, in 'His unutterable plentitude.' In contemplation, the spirit gazes into an abyss, an ocean, a dazzling sun. All concrete conceptions and imaginings, all *corporales similitudines*, are left far behind; banished are all the religious and cultic symbols; even the humanity of the Son of God, the child in the manger, the sufferer on the Cross, are left behind."[52]

of prayer as "the practice of the presence of God," yogis speak of "detachment," Moslems of "surrender." All these expressions and others point to *one* elephant, but an abyss lies between these words and the experience that constitutes their confluence. What does the meditator have if he has no symbols to guide him toward the ineffable goal?

The answer, I think, is twofold: (1) the knowledge of what is *not* his goal, so that he may progress by elimination and outgrowing; and (2) the prompting from his own essence, which sleeps within him and has in its very nature the answers that "he," identifying in himself with his learned roles and cultural heritage, does not know.

The first idea is the backbone of what we shall deal with in the following chapter as "The Negative Way." The second is behind the methods that I describe in Chapter IV as the "Way of Surrender," the "Expressive Way," or the "Way of the Prophets."

3 / The Negative Way

The negative way may seem opposite to the previously described approaches to meditation (upon externally given objects or upon internally arising mental contents), but this is only superficially so. Moreover, *the "negative" dimension of the meditation may be considered to be the invisible backbone sustaining both the concentrative and the expressive way of attunement.* It may be readily seen, in fact, that the concentrative effort involved in meditation upon a *single* object is of an eliminative nature. It is also clear that those forms of meditation involving the development of receptivity toward the unfolding of inner experience imply a passivity possible only through an active effort to eliminate the intrusion of thought on imagination. The practice in "letting go" that this meditation entails, in the sense of "surrendering to" or "allowing," cannot be completely divorced from a letting go in another sense, which is the essence of the negative way: letting go of habits, preconceptions, and expectations; letting go of control and of the filtering mechanisms of ego.

Because the negative or eliminative dimension of meditation is present in both forms implying concentration upon either external or spontaneously emerging "inner" objects (as withdrawal from sensory activity and as passive attention) many of its technical forms coincide with those described in the previous chapter or with those that will be described in the last chapter of this essay. Consequently, I shall concentrate in the following pages on those practices which may be regarded as most characteristic of the negative or eliminative way of approach, and which come, therefore, closest to a pure expression of this direction in spiritual technology.

Yoga is defined by Patanjali at the opening of his sutras as "the *inhibition* of the modifications of the mind." The full accomplishment of this inhibition is attained only in the final stage of samadhi;* however, the eliminative effort is a basic aspect of each one of the "limbs" of yoga, including those that precede meditation proper. I particularly want to stress this aspect in the case of the first two—*yama* and *niyama*—because of the light that this may shed on the spiritual significance of a pervasive aspect of ethics throughout the world.

Yama, the first limb or step of Yoga, comprises vows of abstention or self-restraints: non-violence, non-lying, non-misappropriation, non-craving for sensual enjoyment, non-possessiveness. If we consider the connection between these vows (equivalent to some of the Mosaic commandments) and later phases of yoga, we may understand the broader implications of an extension of meditation into the domain of interpersonal behavior, comparable to the extensions of meditation into ritual philosophy and some art forms considered earlier.

The real point of *yama* is not at all in "morality," as usually understood, in a vision of the good life for society or in the achievement of happiness; but, like Yoga as a whole, in the conquest of the Great Illusion. To this end, the follower of

---

* The term *samadhi* is not employed for a specific state of mind but for a range of "super-conscious" states, which Patanjali classifies in different manners.

this path is required to give up his attachment to the world. *Ahimsa* (non-violence), for instance, is, in its highest expression, utter *transcendence* of the need to harm, and no mere rule of conduct; in the same way *asteya* means not only abstention from stealing, but from misappropriation of privileges, from esteem, from personality traits—a practice in giving up numerous forms of attachment. One function of the external observance of *yama* is to make apparent the subtler aspects of each vow by observing its obvious aspects. It is with inner levels of abstention that the yogi is essentially concerned. Thus, through abstinence from lying he will become more aware of his subtler lies, and in dealing with these he will be able to know his truth and develop intuition. Similarly, by means of a rule of sexual continence he will place himself in a position where he can understand the extent and nature of his cravings for sensuous enjoyment,* and not deceive himself by taking a substitute to be the goal that he really seeks.

In contrast with yama, or self-restraint, *niyama*, the second limb of Yoga, is usually formulated in positive terms. Yet the essence of the observances, like that of the restraints, is detachment, and the eliminative aspect is prominent in both.

Purity, the first observance, is eliminative by definition. As a commentator on Patanjali put it: "Purification means *elimination* from the vehicles belonging to an individual of all those elements and conditions which prevent them from exercising their proper functions and attaining the goal in view...."

Contentment, the second observance, is "the capacity to remain satisfied whatever may happen"; it is based upon "perfect *indifference* to all those personal enjoyments and other considerations which sway mankind." Again, this can only be the outcome

---

* It is important to stress that it is the *craving* for enjoyment and not the enjoyment of the senses itself that yoga seeks to overcome. Pleasure stems from the experience of the present, whereas desire is linked to a projection into the future and suggests a lack of acceptance of the present.

of an eliminative process whereby attachments are relinquished or identification with them transcended.

The third observance, austerity, comprises a variety of practices—fasting, feats of self-discipline, specific vows, etc.—which distinctly involve *privations* of various sorts—food, comfort, sleep, etc. As in the previous observances, the ultimate aim is a condition of equanimity independent from physical, emotional, or even mental satisfactions, a state in which "consciousness abides in itself" and is experienced as independent from all psychophysiological mechanisms. As set forth by Patanjali, Kriya Yoga (the practice of austerity and the remaining two observances, self-study and surrender to God) is practiced for attenuating the *klesas* and bringing about samadhi.

The *klesas*—a term that may be translated as "afflictions" or "roots of pain"—constitute a fundamental aspect of Yoga philosophy and are most relevant to our discussion of the eliminative attitude in meditation. According to Yoga, in fact, the *klesas* are precisely that which *must be eliminated*: ignorance (*avidya*) or lack of awareness of reality; the sense of I-am-ness (*asmita*); attractions and repulsions toward objects; and the desire for life (or fear of death).

Avidya, as explained by Pantanjali, is the root-klesa that causes the self (*atman*), which is unconditioned and eternal, to mistake its true identity. Deprived by maya of the knowledge of its self-sufficient nature, the atman becomes enmeshed in matter and, more particularly, in the flux of his psychological phenomena: perceptions, feelings, thoughts. From this condition derives the second *klesa*, asmita, which Patanjali defines as a blending together of consciousness (*purusa*) and cognition (*buddhi*).

I. K. Taimni remarks in his commentary to the sutras that the word *asmita* derives from *asmi*, which in Sanskrit means "I am":

> "I am" represents the pure awareness of self-existence and is therefore the expression . . . of pure consciousness or the purusa. When the pure consciousness gets involved in matter and, owing to the

power of maya, knowledge of its real nature is lost, the pure "I am" changes into "I am this," where "this" may be the subtlest vehicle through which it is working, or the grossest vehicle, namely, the physical body. The two processes—namely, the loss of awareness of its real nature and the identification with the vehicles—are simultaneous."[1]

Detachment in the context of the yogic world view, when properly understood, is not a matter of less participation in the world, but one that bears on the experience of identity. This becomes clear if one considers that even the overcoming of desires and aversions (which constitute the following *klesas*) is seen as conducive not to inaction but to a different *stance* toward action. The *Bhagavad-Gita*, which is perhaps the most articulate work in the Indian tradition with regard to this subject, describes the attitude of the karma yogin* in terms of *duty*, in contrast with ordinary actions that are dependent upon the pleasure or pain that they bring about. In the latter case, the action is motivated by the attachment or aversion of the doer toward the fruits of his action; in the former, the condition of the doer is such that he experiences each action as its own reward.

Far from being a specific trait of Yoga, the pursuit of detachment is an aspect of every spiritual tradition. Furthermore, in a less technical sense (which has all too frequently led to wrong understanding), detachment is a trait in every major religious system.† It is the marrow of the Christian repudiation of "the world,"‡ for instance, and is inseparable from the Far Eastern formulations of Emptiness. And, just as in Yoga, the practice of detachment in daily life (in the form of vows and observances) constitutes a foundation for the detachment of *ekagrata*, the one-pointedness of the mind required in meditation. In other tradi-

---

* The yogan who follows the discipline of liberation through action.
† Practical asceticism, which may be seen as an unformulated practice in detachment, is also a generalized trait of shamanism.
‡ The *Encyclopedia of Biblical Quotations* lists under "world" nothing but negative pronouncements.

tions, too, the seemingly ethical manifestations of the practice constitute a necessary foundation for a more radical experience of transcendence.

The identity between detachment as an attitude in daily life* and detachment as an attitude in meditation is poignantly conveyed by an episode in the life of Zen Master Bokusan:

> During the civil disturbances of the nineteenth century a fugitive samurai took refuge in the temple of Soto Zen Master Bokusan. Three pursuers arrived and demanded to know where he was. "No one here," said the Zen master. "If you won't tell us, then let's cut off your head," and they drew their swords to do so. "Then if I am to die," said the Zen master, "I think I'll have a little wine." And he took down a small bottle, poured it, and sipped with evident relish.
>
> The samurai looked at one another. Finally they went away.
>
> Bokusan was repeatedly asked about this incident, but did not want to discuss it. Once however he said: "Well, there is something to be learnt from it. When those fellows came, I did not do what they wanted, but neither did I quarrel with them or plead with them. I just gave up their whole world and had nothing to do with them. And after a time I found they had gone away.
>
> "Similarly when people complain that they are overwhelmed with passions and wrong thoughts, they should know that the right way is not to quarrel nor to plead or argue. Simply give up all claim on their world and have nothing to do with them, and after a time you will find that they have gone away."[2]

Seen from without, the negative way can be easily taken to express a hateful denial of joy, of nature, and of the human body. This misinterpretation is more than understandable, since the outward actions that constitute such a discipline in different lands have served for centuries as a channel for a collective aber-

* A cross-cultural examination of spiritual exercises involving detachment in action would probably be an endeavor of no less scope than the present one on meditation techniques—ranging from painful puberty ordeals to sophisticated exercises in dis-identification.

ration. Fear, inhibition, self-hate, shame, guilt—they all find expression and apparent justification in the "virtuous" front provided by a life of "renunciation." It was to this psycho-pathological trait in the Western world that Nietzsche addressed himself through his Zarathustra when he said that those who talk of celestial hopes are poisoners, whether they know it or not:

> Offending God was once the greatest offense, but God died and with him died his offenders. To offend the earth is now the dreadest thing: to esteem the entrails of the unknowable higher than the aim of the earth! Once the soul looked down contemptuously at the body; the greatest thing of all was this contempt. The soul wanted the body lean, hideous, starved. By such means it sought to escape the body and the earth. Oh, but that soul was itself lean, hideous, and starved: cruelty was the debauchery of that soul.[3]

In spite of historically prevalent forms of pseudo-detachment, pseudo-humility, pseudo-serenity, etc. (where these and other classical "virtues" have become *tokens* of virtue in a purely extrinsic sense altogether incompatible with their true nature), it is not difficult to see that these false interpretations derive their very existence from a true model. Detachment, serenity, and purity (to choose the more denying of them all) are aspects of that ideal condition of the psyche that we have seen as being the aim of meditation and that we have been examining from different angles.

A measure of non-attachment is the source of a healthy individual's ability to stand on his own, not mistaking his identity with that of an owner of given things or a performer of a certain role. It is also the source of a basic independence from others, which is, in turn, the prerequisite for true relationships. A measure of non-attachment to one's own moods and whims is involved in that attitude of psychological health which we define as "ego strength"—the ability to stand above oneself—which goes hand in hand with the capacity to accept pain, discomfort, and frustration rather than repress or avoid them. More radically than any standard of mental health, though, the negative way

arises from an implicit acknowledgement that man's optimal state
of consciousness is one of *total* detachment: such total surrender
of man to his cosmic duty that not even attachment to life or
fear of death can deviate him from his path. In terms of such
an aspiration we cannot be surprised at the small and great degree
of unpleasantness imposed by styles of meditation in which this
component predominates.*

The practice that tackles most directly the question of not
doing (and the underlying ego annihilation) is one that cannot
properly be called a technique:

> This Ch'an† is the supreme Ch'an of seeing one's Buddha-nature
> instantly. But if this is so, why should one bother to practice the
> so-called Seven Days' Meditation? [You must understand that]
> people's capacity to practice the dharma is deteriorating all the
> time. Nowadays people have too many distracting thoughts in their
> minds. Therefore the Patriarchs have designed special methods and
> techniques. . . ."   —Discourse of Master Hsu Yun.[4]

Among the techniques, though, none comes closer to being
a pure expression of wu-wei (non-action) than that which Japanese Zen calls shikan-taza, a term approximately translated as "just
sitting."

Not long ago, Shrinyu Suzuki Roshi, the abbot of Tassajara
Zen Monastery in Big Sur, California, was invited to Stanford
University to demonstrate Zen meditation. He laid his pillow on
the floor, bowed in salutation to it, sat, and then explained that
in Za-Zen the back is held straight, the ears in a line with the
shoulders, the hands are placed over the belly, forming a
mudra—as he was indicating—the eyes, half closed, are focused
on a spot about three feet in front of the meditator. Thereupon
he started to meditate and did not address his audience again

---

* Some of the martial arts of the Far East, the theme of which is—from
one point of view—the cultivation of serenity, may literally involve the
confrontation of death.
† "Ch'an" is the Chinese equivalent for "Zen," from which the latter,
Japanese expression derives.

until the end of an hour, when he bowed to the people remaining and departed.

If Suzuki Roshi's non-lecture is not explicit enough, perhaps its message may be brought into the light by statements that he has voiced on other occasions. Some of his statements may be intriguing or not understandable at all to one unacquainted with Zen or the experiences with which Zen deals. Nevertheless they come closer to explaining the inner dimension of "just sitting" than any scholarly and logically careful exposition could. The following excerpts are from a lecture he delivered during a sesshin in the summer of 1966:

"Most of you are beginners, so it may be rather difficult for you to understand why we practice Za-Zen or meditation in this way. We always say, 'just sit,' and if you do, you will find out that Zen practice—just to sit—is not so easy. Just to sit may be the most difficult thing. To work on something is not difficult; but not to work on anything is rather difficult. When we have the idea of 'self,' we want some reason why we work on something. But if you do not have any idea of self, we want some reason why we work on something. But if you do not have any idea of self, you can remain silent and calm whether or not you work on something. You will not lose your composure. So to remain silent and calm is a kind of test you will receive. If you can do it, it means you have no idea of self. If your life is based on the usual idea of self, what you do will not be successful in its true sense. It will be success in one way, but in another you are digging your own grave. So to work without the idea of self is a very important one. It is much more important than making a good decision. Even a good decision based on a one-sided idea of self will create difficulties for yourself and others. . . .

"All the difficulties you have in Za-Zen should not take place outside your mind. Your efforts should be kept within your mind. In other words, you have to accept the difficulty of not being other than what you are. You should not try to make some tentative particular efforts based on your small mind—like, 'My practice should be better.' *My* practice, you say, but Za-Zen is not your practice. It is Buddha's practice. Your effort is based on big mind, which you cannot get out of. If your small self begins to act without the care of big mind, that is not Zen. What you should do should be well taken care of by big mind."⁵

And at a lecture at Zen Mountain Center, in 1968, Suzuki said:

"I want to explain shikan-taza, what it means *just to sit*. Some monks said to a Zen master, 'It is very hard. How is it possible to sit somewhere where there is no hot and no cold weather?'" The master answered, 'When it is hot, you should be hot Buddha. When it is cold, you should be cold Buddha.' This is Dogen Zenji's understanding of the story. Actually, the master said, 'When it is hot, you should kill hot. When it is cold, you should kill cold.' But if you say, *kill*, the *kill* is extra. If you say to obtain enlightenment, the *obtain* is extra. Dogen was very direct when he said, 'When it is hot, you should be hot Buddha. When it is cold, you should be cold Buddha.' That is what shikan-taza, just to sit, means.

"When your practice is not good, you are poor Buddha. When your practice is good, you are good Buddha. And *poor* and *good* are Buddhas themselves. *Poor* is Buddha and *good* is Buddha and *you* are Buddha also. Whatever you think, say, every word becomes Buddha. I am Buddha. *I* is Buddha, and *am* is Buddha, and *Buddha* is Buddha. Buddha. Buddha. Buddha. Buddha. Whatever you say. Then there are no problems. There is no need to translate it into English, no need to be bothered with fancy explanations of Buddhism. Everything is Buddha: lying down is Buddha, each word is Buddha. If you say Buddhabuddhabuddhabuddhabuddha, that is our way, that is shikan-taza. When you practice Za-Zen with this understanding, that is true Za-Zen. Even though we say just to sit, to understand it is difficult, and that may be why Dogen Zenji left us so many teachings. But this does not mean that the teachings are difficult. When you sit, you know what he means without thinking and without expecting anything from it. When you accept yourself as a Buddha, or accept everything as an unfolding of the absolute teaching, the truth, the first principle, or as a part of the great being, when you reach this understanding, whatever you think or see is the actual teaching of Buddha and whatever you do is the actual practice of Buddha. Problems arise because you are trying to do something, or because you think that nothing will arise because of doing something, or because you feel that you can rely on something. . . .

"Masters who understand the Soto way may give you the koan *Mu* instead of telling you just to sit. *Just to sit!* There is no difference and *just to sit* will be various kinds of koans. There may be thousands of koans, and just to sit includes them all. This is the direct way to enlightenment, liberation, nirvana, or whatever you say."[6]

Another form of meditation involving the negative approach to a high degree is that known in Buddhism as "insight meditation" or the *vipassana method* (in contrast to absorptive meditation, which leads to the jhanas—trance states characterized by a suspension of thought and tranquility rather than insight).

The practice of the vipassana method, although amply described in Buddhist texts, was apparently forgotten until this century, when the Burmese monk Mahasi Sayadaw "rediscovered" it, and taught it. Presently it is the dominant form of meditation in Burma, and from that country it is spreading to other Buddhist centers of the world.[7]

The term "insight" (vipassana) used to designate this method may be misleading, for it tends to suggest an active intellectual pursuit, which is not part of this technique. The practice is designed to lead the meditator to insight into the "three characteristics of existence": impermanence (*anicca*), suffering and insufficiency (*dukkha*), and impersonality (*anatta*). Yet this insight, which will crown his practice, is not the fruit of discursive thought but of *direct observation* of experience.

The basis of the vipassana method is in the practice of what Buddhist scriptures call "right-mindfulness" or "foundations of mindfulness." Right-mindfulness is the seventh factor of the "eightfold path leading to the extinction of suffering," which itself constitutes the fourth of the Four Noble Truths of Buddhism.

Right-mindfulness rests upon two faculties called in Buddhist texts "bare attention" and "clear comprehension." Sometimes, however, "mindfulness, (*sati*) is used in association with the expression "clear comprehension" (*sampajanna*), and in such instances, as Nyaponika Thera has pointed out, "mindfulness applies pre-eminently to the attitude and practice of bare attention and a purely receptive state of mind."

"Bare attention" provides the key to the distinctive methods of satipatthana, and "accompanies the systematic practice from its very beginning to the achievement of its highest goals." It is in bare attention that we find the characteristic orientation of the *negative way*.

The very expression "*bare* attention" indicates the eliminative aspect of the practice, which consists in the mere registering of sense impressions, feelings, or mental states "without reacting to them by deed, speech, or mental comment. . . . By cultivating a receptive state of mind, which is the first stage in the process of perception, bare attention *cleans* the mind, and prepares the mind for subsequent mental processes." The cleansing aspect of the practice is repeatedly stressed in the Pali texts. The foundations of mindfulness are "for the purification of beings."

Bare attention, which might be thought of as a mental operation leading to an impoverishment of experience, may, on the contrary, reveal the complexity of the world when not masked by our simplifying labels. Nyaponika Thera comments that the individual

will first find out that, where he believes himself to be dealing with a unity, *i.e.*, with a single object presented by a single act of perception, there is multiplicity, *i.e.*, the whole series of physical and mental processes presented by corresponding acts of perception, following each other in quick succession. He will further notice with consternation how rarely he is aware of a bare or pure object without any alien admixture. For instance, the normal visual perception, if it is of evidence of any interest to the observer, will rarely present the visual object pure and simple, but the object will appear in the light of added subjective judgments: beautiful or ugly, pleasant or unpleasant, useful, useless, or harmful. If it concerns a living being, there will also enter into the preconceived notion: this is a personality, an égo, just as "I" am, too! . . . It is the task of bare attention to *eliminate** all those alien additions from the object proper that is then in the field of perception.[8]

How bare attention may be the foundation of insight is suggested by the statement (in the commentary to the Sutta Nipata) that "only things well examined by Mindfulness can be understood by Wisdom, but not confused ones." Also, "bare attention first allows things to speak for themselves, without interrupting." This injunction implies very specially the suppression of fantasy or daydreaming, "which by its tough and sticky substance of endlessly repetitive character crowds the narrow space of present consciousness giving no chance for its shaping, and making it, in fact, still more shapeless and slack."

The outline of the vipassana method is summed up in the opening of Buddha's discourse on the foundations of mindfulness—the Maha Satipatthana Sutta.

The four areas of contemplation indicated in the quoted text quoted above—the body, the feelings, the mind, and mind-objects—are treated in detail in the rest of the sutra. Mindfulness of the body, for instance, comprises mindfulness of breathing, mindfulness of postures and movements, and several exercises in which the meditator contemplates the body from specific points of view. The practice of breathing meditation (*anapana sati*) is a cornerstone of the whole method and is dealt with in detail in the Vinaya and the Sutta Pitakas (the instructions are also included in Buddhaghosa's "Path of Purification").

I have already described in Chapter 1 a modified form of the

* Italics the author's.

practice of mindful breathing, introduced in modern times by
the Burmese meditation master Mahasi Sayadaw. In this exercise
the meditator attends to the sensations of the rising and falling of
the abdomen rather than to the tactile sensations of air passing
through the nose, as described in the sutras. Just as it was appropriate to discuss this method in connection with the role
of concentrated attention in meditation, it will be a relevant
illustration of the principle of spontaneity and relinquishment of
intentional control, which is the subject matter of Chapter 4.
This points up the statement made at the beginning of this
chapter that the negative approach is not only compatible with
the other two dimensions of meditation, but constitutes their
backbone.

Just as the absorptive aspect of meditation has its parallel
in contemporary psychotherapy, so the negative aspect has a
parallel, which is striking because of its resemblance to the
satipatthana method: the exercise of the "awareness continuum"
in Gestalt therapy.

As in the Buddhist practice of mindfulness, the object of this
exercise that is central to Gestalt therapy is simple awareness.
The creator of the method, Frederick S. Perls, even insisted:
awareness of the *obvious*. As in the satipatthana method, awareness of the obvious involves suppression of fantasy, minimization
of conceptual activity, and the elimination of anticipation or
reminiscences. "I have one aim only," says Perls, "to impart a
fraction of the meaning of the word *now*. To me, nothing
exists except the now. Now = experience = awareness = reality.
The past is no more and the future not yet." Compare this with
Nyaponika Thera's statement: "Right-mindfulness recovers for
man the lost pearl of his freedom, snatching it from the jaws of
the dragon Time. Right-mindfulness cuts men loose from the
fetters of the past, which he foolishly tries even to re-enforce by
looking back frequently, with eyes of longing, resentment, or
regret. Right-mindfulness stops man from chaining himself even

now to the imaginations of his fears and hopes, to anticipated events of the future. Thus, right-mindfulness restores to man a freedom that is to be found only in the present."[9]

The difference between Gestalt therapy and the satipatthana method is that in the former the exercise in awareness is verbalized, and this makes supervision possible. It is precisely such corrective supervision that makes it, more than an awareness training (as it is sometimes called), a *therapy*.

Other than pointing out the connection the Gestalt therapeutic exercise with meditation in general (for it is an exercise in awareness) and, specifically, with the negative way (for it involves the elimination of thought, fantasy, memory, and anticipation), I will not say more of the psychotherapeutic procedure.[10]

4 / The Way of Surrender
and Self-Expression

The way of Za-Zen may be regarded as the way of surrender of personal preferences: an emptying oneself of preconceptions (in the intellectual aspects), greed (in the emotional), and self-will, in order to discover that enlightenment bypasses or is not dependent on the satisfactions of those habits that we call our personality. As well as the movement of surrender or letting go *of* something, we can also see that there is place in meditation for an attitude of surrender *to*.

This might seem an attempt doomed to failure, if we consider that any surrender to our preferences is likely to leave us subject to those impulses in our personality that constitute the very prison or vicious circle that we want to transcend. If saying "No" to our little ego proves to be effective, could saying "Yes" to it be effective as well? In this, as in other things, paradoxes seem to be more compatible with empirical reality than with logical reasoning, and experience indicates that surrender *to* impulse may not be the blind alley that it seems to be.

An anecdote may be appropriate here to suggest how a respectful attitude toward the spontaneous urge of the moment may become a key to the meditation process. This is a story about an ancient Hindu king who was very attached to his riches, and yet, having developed a feeling of the nothingness of his vast wealth, was eager to meditate in order to apprehend the timeless reality. A yogi gave the king instructions:

The king sat down to meditate in earnest, but whenever he tried to fix his mind upon the eternal, it went blank. Pretty soon, without his knowing it, his imagination began to hover around his beautiful bracelet, of which he was particularly fond. Before his admiring gaze, the real bracelet began to sparkle in all the colors of the rainbow. As soon as he found himself in that fantasy, he fought his way back to God. But the harder he tried to fix his mind upon God, the bigger was the disappointment he experienced. God invariably changed in his mind into the bracelet. With much humility, the king now went to the yogi for further instructions. The yogi knew how to turn the weakness itself into a source of strength. He said to the king, "Since your mind is so much attached to the bracelet, start right there. Meditate upon the bracelet. Contemplate its beauty and gorgeous colors. Then inquire into the source of that beauty and those colors. The bracelet is, in its objective essence, a configuration of energy vibrations. It is the perceptive mind which lends it its beauty and color. Therefore, try to understand the nature of the mind which created the world as you see it."[1]

The decision to meditate upon the bracelet, in this story, aligns with what we have called the way of descent, the contemplation of individual aspects of reality rather than of its unity—in symbol or direct experience. Although the king's greater attraction toward his precious object removes him from the One and draws him to one of the Hundred Thousand Things, is not each of these worldly objects also an echo of the One?

In contrast to the way of detachment, which would have us see the whole world as maya, we may instead develop an attitude of reverence toward all of existence, and trust in the compass that life has placed in our hearts. If we thus follow our feelings, rather than constrain them, we are most likely to find that our preferences of today become obsolete in the face of tomorrow's; the music that we now enjoy, the books that nourish us, the women or men that we feel in resonance with, may become trite, exhausted of meaning, too obvious or shallow to our future perceptions, likings, and needs. Yet that shift of attitude, which would make our present feelings seem indiscriminate or lacking in orientation, would have taken place precisely through satiation, not through denial. Just as in life we grow by outgrowing, and we outgrow by living something out completely, our perceptions may be refined by giving in to our inner voices to the fullest degree.

Athough the attitudes called for by the concentrative and by the receptive ways appear as perfectly logical opposites, this need not be so in actual experience. It would be better to view them as divergent ways that converge upon the same goal. They may be experienced as divergent at the beginning of the journey but as aspects of the same attitude when the meditator is approaching higher states of consciousness. In these, empathy with an attractive object leads to a state of desirelessness—the very gratuitousness of beauty and detachment makes the world more alive and not dead. As Ch'an Master Hsu Yun has put it: "Oh, friends and disciples, if you do not attach yourselves to the Ten Thousand Things with your minds, you will find that the life-spark will emanate from *everything*."[2]

The borderline between the negative attitude of "just sitting" and that of surrendering to experience is a very delicate one indeed, and one that may be discerned most clearly in the case of visions, revelations, physical sensations that commonly take place in meditation. In the Japanese Zen tradition, these are all called *makyo* (meaning "diabolical phenomena"), and while not considered inherently bad, they are regarded as a potential obstacle to Za-Zen. According to the Za-Zen Yojinki, "The disciple may develop the faculty of seeing through solid objects as though they were transparent, or he may experience his own body as a translucent substance. He may see Buddhas and Bodhisattvas. Penetrating insights may suddenly come to him, or passages of sutras which were particularly difficult to understand may suddenly become luminously clear to him. Yet," the book goes on to say, "these abnormal visions and sensations are merely the symptoms of an impairment arising from a maladjustment of the mind with the breath."[3]

The indifference of Zen masters to these phenomena may be surprising to the disciple, and hard to understand for anyone not familiar with the Way of Emptiness. *Makyo* may be experienced as highly rewarding and desirable, and are valued in other religions. Yet this attitude of Zen toward unusual contents of consciousness does not differ from its attitude with regard to contents of consciousness in general—the aim being awareness of awareness in itself: the direct grasping of mind by mind.* This was made explicit by Yasutani Roshi, the Japanese Zen master who has lectured extensively in the United States. He has pointed out that makyo has a general as well as a specific sense:

> Broadly speaking, the entire life of the ordinary man is nothing but makyo. Even such Bodhisattvas as Monju and Kannon, highly developed though they are, still have about them traces of makyo; otherwise they would be supreme Buddhas, completely free of makyo. One who becomes attached to what he realizes through satori is also still lingering in the world of makyo. So, you see, there are makyo even after enlightenment. . . ."[4]

The attitude that is recommended in face of makyo is therefore no different from that which characterizes Zen in general: detached awareness. The issue deserves special mention only because the exceptional nature of the phenomena might seem to

* The word *hsin*, frequently translated as "mind," may be rendered also by "heart" or "consciousness."

call for an exception. For instance, cases are reported of persons who have written down things that turned out to be prophetically true, or who felt in communication with divine beings. The Zen view of these states, though, is that they constitute a mixture of reality and unreality, falling short of true enlightenment. They indicate progress in the practice of meditation, and yet they would not be part of a more concentrated state.

> Just as dreams do not appear to a person in deep sleep but only when he is half-asleep and half-awake, so makyo do not come to those in deep concentration or samadhi. Never be tempted into thinking that these phenomena are real or that the visions themselves have any meaning. To see a beautiful vision of a Bodhisattva does not mean that you are any nearer becoming one yourself, any more than a dream of being a millionaire means that you are any richer when you awake. Hence there is no reason to feel elated about such makyo. And similarly, whatever horrible monsters may appear to you, there is no cause whatever for alarm. Above all, do not allow yourself to be enticed by visions of the Buddha or of gods blessing you or communicating a divine message, or by makyo involving prophecies which turn out to be true. This is to squander your energies in the foolish pursuit of superstition.[5]

These very phenomena against which Zen warns its followers as deceptive surrogates of enlightenment are the substance of the trance states cultivated by the alternative approach to meditation. The domain of surrender or letting go is typically that of visionary experience, automatic movements, the release of dormant physical energies, inspired utterance, automatic writing, spirit possession.

Yet if we consider these superficially contrasting attitudes closely enough, we may see where they meet. On one hand, the way of detachment, in its ripeness, cannot help being permissive; a suppressive effort would entail attachment to a preference or perception and would fall short of non-action. (It is no coincidence that makyo appear in Za-Zen. This is because this system cultivates a state of undistracted receptivity, and though the meditator is warned not to become attached to his visions, he is not told to suppress them but to persist in the stance of both not doing and allowing, which characterizes Shikan-taza.) On the other hand, a complete surrender cannot fail to involve detachment, for a greedy interest in the attainment of certain mental states would cease to be surrender altogether. We might say that there is a condition of *openness to experience,* expressed by both detachment and surrender.

In the actual experience of meditation, though, this meeting point of detachment and surrender may take a long time to attain. And so we see, in its less perfected stages, a sharp contrast between a dry asceticism of the mind* and a tumultuous Dionysian spirit; between the serene spirit of the monk and the seeming madness of the prophet; between the pursuit of emptiness and the phenomena of possession by gods or cosmic forces.

Possession by gods, spirits, or energies is, indeed, the most characteristic experience in the domain of spirituality that we are discussing at this point, just as an equanimity transcending all feeling and thought is most characteristic of the Apollonian way (see Figure 1, p. 16). Possession also differs from the absorptive way of meditation insofar as in possession there is no *union* of subject and object† (which the word *samadhi* reflects—*sam,* meaning "together" or "with" in Sanskrit), but a state in which the subject entirely disappears and becomes a mere channel. As in the case of the individual in absorption he may say, "I am God," but it is not he but the entity speaking through him that says "I." Also, in spite of the abysmal difference between a possession state and the ordinary state of hypnotic trance, it seems legitimate to inquire as to whether both depend on a similar propensity within the person to be in a dissociated state—*i.e.,* a state in which the habitual role, style, and center of consciousness are relinquished, and a different personality role, style, and state of consciousness

---

* As in countless instances among the Fathers of the Desert in Christianity and in the history of Hinayana Buddhism.
† See quotations pp. 28–29 and pp. 30–31.

are adopted, frequently without knowledge or memory of this having happened.

When contrasting the orgiastic-prophetic dimension of the revelatory state with the dimension of detachment and equanimity that we discussed before, we may say that the main difference between them is the importance ascribed to *content*. Everything the Zen monk would consider makyo—imagery, feelings, voices, etc.—here is likely to become the very goal of the meditation. The inner vision, idea, or inspired utterance of the shaman, sybil, or prophet, is frequently regarded not as a by-product of an individual quest but as a self-sufficient end of one's function in the community: a channel for revelation.

From this angle we may also contrast the revelatory and concentrative ways of meditation. While both forms are content-centered, they differ (especially in the degraded forms of each) in the relative accent placed on the social or individual role (product versus person, message versus state), and, more radically, in the contrast between the structural content of the former and the unstructured, inwardly determined content of the latter. While a Christian may attempt to apply the idea of death and resurrection to his own life and inwardly enact an "imitation of Christ," the Dionysian Bacchae would abandon themselves unconditionally to the workings of their deeper nature, there to find, without seeking it, the eternal rhythm of death and resurrection.

Perhaps the best illustration for much of what I have been saying is to be found in shamanism, which, as a whole, embodies the orgiastic-revelatory aspect of experience as much as Buddhism embodies the dimension of emptiness. Not only is shamanism in general a mysticism of possession, but the shaman's trance is usually content-oriented. A shaman* that may properly be called

* The shaman performs the roles of priest, medicine-man, prophet, artist, and is not to be confused with the formal priest or medicine-man who exists in some cultures in addition to the shaman. What distinguishes the shaman is his ability to "transport himself to other worlds", *i.e.*, to experience altered states of consciousness.

so is not a seeker of enlightenment or an individual who indulges in altered states of consciousness as part of a discipline for personal development. He is one who has attained communication with the supernatural (a spirit world, in most shamanistic conceptions) and may act as a mediator between spirits or gods and man, making the desires of each known to the other. In this, he may be called a primitive prophet. Apparently his ecstasy is not for himself but for others: his patients, his disciples, or the community at large. Yet we must not forget that in his becoming a mouthpiece of the gods he fulfills *his* calling—and some reports indicate that a shaman that has no occasion to shamanize tends to become ill.

In no instance better than in that of shamanism can we discern the archetypal—inwardly prompted—nature of the symbols that later religions have crystallized into standard forms.

Ideas such as the journey to the underworld, ascent to heaven, death and resurrection, are not mere *ideas* in shamanism but actual experiences that are renewed generation after generation. In countries as far apart as Australia, South America, and the Arctic Circle, these are echoed with the same freshness of spirit. Constancies such as these are generally interpreted as an indication of a shamanistic "tradition," spread by migrations. But do we not overstate, perhaps, the necessity of tradition in our experiential ignorance of the archetypal domain? It is quite possible that the essence of the tradition may lie in a tradition of no-tradition: the fostering of an openness (which perhaps is more easy in pre-industrial cultures than in ours) whereby the individual can discover in himself all that his ancestors did not enforce upon his world view. Consider, for instance, the following account of his initiatory experience by a Siberian shaman who, far from seeking it, plunged into it with no apparent expectations:

A. A. Popov gives the following account concerning a shaman of the Avam Samoyed. Sick with smallpox, the future shaman remained unconscious for three days and so nearly dead that on the

third day he was almost buried. His initiation took plàce during
the time. He remembered having been carried into the middle
of a sea. There he heard his Sickness (that is, smallpox) speak,
saying to him: "From the Lords of the Water you will receive
the gift of shamanizing. Your name as a shaman will be Huottarie
(Diver)." Then the Sickness troubled the water of the sea. The
candidate came out and climbed a mountain. There he met a naked
woman and began to suckle at her breast. The woman, who was
probably the Lady of the Water, said to him: "You are my child;
that is why I let you suckle at my breast. You will meet many
hardships and be greatly wearied." The husband of the Lady of
the Water, the Lord of the Underworld, then gave him two guides,
an ermine and a mouse, to lead him to the underworld. When they
came to a high place, the guides showed him seven tents with
torn roofs. He entered the first and there found the inhabitants
of the underworld and the men of the Great Sickness (syphilis).
These men tore out his heart and threw it into a pot. In other
tents he met the Lord of Madness and the Lords of all the nervous
disorders, as well as the evil shamans. Thus he learned the various
diseases that torment mankind.

Still preceded by his guides, the candidate then came to the Land
of the Shamanesses, who strengthened his throat and his voice.
He was then carried to the shores of the Nine Seas. In the middle
of one of them was an island, and in the middle of the island a
young birch tree rose to the sky. It was the Tree of the Lord
of the Earth. Beside it grew nine herbs, the ancestors of all the
plants on earth. The tree was surrounded by seas, and in each of
these swam a species of bird with its young. There were several
kinds of ducks, a swan, and a sparrow-hawk. The candidate
visited all these seas; some of them were salt, others so hot he
could not go near the shore. After visiting the seas, the candidate
raised his head and, in the top of the tree, saw men of various
nations: Tavgi Samoyed, Russians, Dolgan, Yakut, and Tungus. He
heard voices: "It has been decided that you shall have a drum (that
is, the body of a drum) from the branches of this tree." He began
to fly with the birds of the seas. As he left the shore, the Lord of
the Tree called to him: "My branch has just fallen; take it and

make a drum of it that will serve you all your life." The branch
had three forks, and the Lord of the Tree bade him make three
drums from it, to be kept by three women, each drum being for
a special ceremony—the first for shamanizing woman in child-
birth, the second for curing the sick, the third for finding men
lost in the snow.

The Lord of the Tree also gave branches to all the men who
were in the top of the tree. But, appearing from the tree up to the
chest in human form, he added: "One branch only I give not to the
shamans, for I keep it for the rest of mankind. They can make
dwellings from it and so use it for their needs. I am the Tree
that gives life to all men." Clasping the branch, the candidate
was ready to resume his flight when again he heard a human
voice, this time revealing to him the medicinal virtues of the seven
plants and giving him certain instructions concerning the art of
shamanizing. But, the voice added, he must marry three women
(which, in fact, he later did by marrying three orphan girls whom
he had cured of smallpox).

And after that he came to an endless sea and there he found
trees and seven stones. The stones spoke to him one after the
other. The first had teeth like bears' teeth and a basket-shaped
cavity, and it revealed to him that it was the earth's holding stone;
it pressed on the fields with its weight, so that they should not be
carried away by the wind. The second served to melt iron. He
remained with these stones for seven days and so learned how they
could be of use to men.

Then his two guides, the ermine and the mouse, led him to a
high, rounded mountain. He saw an opening before him and
entered a bright cave, covered with mirrors, in the middle of
which there was something like a fire. He saw two women, naked
but covered with hair, like reindeer. Then he saw that there was no
fire burning but that the light came from above, through an
opening. One of the women told him that she was pregnant and
would give birth to two reindeer; one would be the sacrificial
animal of the Dolgan and Evenki, the other that of the Tavgi.
She also gave him a hair, which was to be useful to him when
he shamanized for reindeer. The other woman also gave birth to

two reindeer, symbols of the animals that would aid man in all his works and also supply his food. The cave had two openings, toward the north and toward the south; through each of them the young women sent a reindeer to serve the forest people (Dolgan and Evenki). The second woman, too, gave him a hair. When he shamanizes, he mentally turns toward the cave.

Then the candidate came to a desert and saw a distant mountain. After three days' travel he reached it, entered an opening, and came upon a naked man working a bellows. On the fire was a cauldron "as big as half the earth." The naked man saw him and caught him with a huge pair of tongs. The novice had time to think, "I am dead!" The man cut off his head, chopped his body into bits, and put everything in the cauldron. There he boiled his body for three years. There were also three anvils, and the naked man forged the candidate's head on the third, which was the one on which the best shamans were forged. Then he threw the head into one of three pots that stood there, the one in which the water was the coldest. He now revealed to the candidate that, when he was called to cure someone, if the water in the ritual pot was very hot, it would be useless to shamanize, for the man was already lost; if the water was warm, he was sick but would recover; cold water denoted a healthy man.

The blacksmith then fished the candidate's bones out of a river, in which they were floating, put them together, and covered them with flesh again. He counted them and told him that he had three too many; he was therefore to procure three shaman's costumes. He forged his head and taught him how to read the letters that are inside it. He changed his eyes; and that is why, when he shamanizes, he does not see with his bodily eyes but with these mystical eyes. He pierced his ears, making him able to understand the language of plants. Then the candidate found himself on the summit of a mountain, and finally he woke in the yurt, among the family. Now he can sing and shamanize indefinitely, without ever growing tired.[6]

The resemblance between shamanistic experience and the mystic experiences encountered in the "higher religions" goes beyond mere content, striking as this aspect may be (cf., death-resurrection theme in Osiris, Attis, Adonis, in the Tibetan Tchöd ritual, and the journeys to the other world of Aeneas, Enoch, Mohammed, St. Paul, and others). Also, the psychological character of the shamanistic experience is fairly constant and is the prototype of that which we recognize in prophets and other inspired men of more recent cultures. The aspect of the shamanistic experience is one that the individual expresses either as a separation of the soul from the body (so that it may visit other places and levels of existence), or as a penetration of his soul-free body by other spirits (animal, demonic, or angelic); possibly, by both at the same time. The Greeks gave names to these two concepts: the flight from the body they called ἔκστασις (ecstasy), and the penetration by the spirits, ἔνθεος (enthusiasm—literally, "in God," or "God within"). The quality that inspires such interpretations seems to link together experiences that are remote in time, place, or cultural setting. The resemblances may be even more apparent from the frequent physical or visible concomitants of this type of experience: the seer's frenzy, his seeming madness taking the form of agitation, his convulsive movements, glossalalia,* lack of regard for his social image or physical safety, followed by a period of calm and, later, of forgetfulness for the whole event. Compare, for instance, the following descriptions:

Even as she spoke, neither her features nor her complexion remained the same, nor was her hair confined within her braid; her bosom heaved, and her wild heart was stolen with frenzy; her stature was longer to the sight, her voice no longer human: so soon she was inspired by the breath of the god as it came ever nearer . . . at length no longer submitting herself to Phoebus, the prophetess rages furiously in her cavern, if so be, she may succeed in flinging off the mighty god from her bosom. All the more he plies her frenzied mouth, subduing her wild heart and fashions her to his will by constraint.—*Aeneid*, Book vi.

* From the Greek, "speaking in tongues."

[When David fled to Samuel for protection] Saul sent messengers to take David: and when they saw the company of the prophets prophesying, and Samuel standing as appointed over them, the Spirit of God was upon the messengers of Saul, and they also prophesied. [Saul sent messengers three times,] then went he also to Ramah . . . and the Spirit of God was upon him also, and he went on, and prophesied, until he came to Naioth in Ramah. And he stripped off his clothes also, and prophesied before Samuel in like manner, and lay down naked all that day and all that night.
—I Samuel 19

And when the day of Pentecost was fully come, they were all with one accord in one place. And suddenly there came a sound from heaven as of a rushing, mighty wind, and it filled all the houses where they were sitting. And there appeared unto them cloven tongues like as of fire, and it sat upon each of them. And they were all filled with the Holy Ghost, and began to speak with other tongues, as the Spirit gave them utterance. And there were dwelling at Jerusalem Jews, devout men, out of every nation under heaven. . . . And they were all amazed, and were in doubt, saying one to another, What meaneth this? Others mocking said, These men are full of new wine.
—Acts of the Apostles 2

In spite of the constancy of the characteristic of the possession trance, however, it seems necessary to draw a distinction between states of greater or lesser *quality*, in terms of the level of experience to which they relate, or the excellence of their content. This distinction is acknowledged in all cultures and attributed to the nature of the entities by whom the individual is possessed. Islamic thought, for instance, draws a distinction between inspiration by jinn or by angels, and Mahomet himself is said to have distrusted his own states at the beginning, regarding them as the workings of jinn rather than divine revelation. Even among jinn, distinctions in quality are drawn. Whereas some are regarded as the inspirers of poets or of soothsayers (*'arraf*, who sometimes gives his oracles in verse), others inspire the less profound utterances of the diviner (*kahin*, who will give inspiration on practical issues such as the finding of lost objects).*

Though frequently the individual will maintain connections with a specific entity (jinni, spirit helper, "familiar spirit," etc., according to the tradition), or with entities at a given level of mystical realization, there are exceptions in the instances of shamans who declare themselves to be in contact with *many* spirit helpers and who will attend to matters as different in scope as divination related to hunting and the leading of the souls of the dead. Even in the case of such a High Prophet as Elisha, we find an instance in which he was asked for an oracle on where to find a water supply:

> . . . And it came to pass, when the minstrel played, that the hand of the Lord came upon him.
>
> And he said, Thus saith the Lord, Make this valley full of ditches.
>
> For thus saith the Lord, Ye shall not see wind, neither shall ye see rain; yet that valley shall be filled with water, that ye may drink, both ye, and your cattle, and your beasts.
>
> —II Kings 3

Not only can we discern differences in "level" among instances of revelation, ranging from the stage clairvoyant to the prophet, but differences in quality at a given level—stylistic differences that might be likened to the different colors of the spectrum.

Plutarch draws this distinction for us when he classifies inspiration or "enthusiasm" into the diviner, prompted by Apollo; the Bacchic frenzy, prompted by Dionysus, Cybele, and Pan; the warlike frenzy of Ares; the poet's frenzy, inspired by the Muses; and the most fiery of all, the frenzy of love.[7]

---

* To the more orthodox Muslims, only the Prophet is regarded as divinely possessed—his words being inspired by the Archangel Gabriel. In this we see the tendency of all orthodoxies to substitute the realization of the individual for that of the savior, rather than seeing their highest exemplar as the embodiment of a universal ideal and possibility. Thus, other instances of God-incarnation in the Moslem world (like the Sufi Hallaj) were considered heretical.

Today we may want to call the Greek gods "archetypes," regarding them, as Jung puts it, as "organs of the psyche"[8] comparable to those in our body. Notwithstanding this shift in point of view (which turns the gods from personalities to forces within us), Plutarch's classification holds for what we know of possession in all cultures, regardless of the names or interpretations given to these states.

One last important distinction is that drawn by many cultures with regard to the good or the evil nature of possessing entities.

At least in the Judeo-Christian and Moslem worlds, the tendency to interpret all possession as caused by devils or the Devil seems to have run parallel to the establishment of a formalized orthodoxy. Whereas jinn appear to have been regarded as amoral in early times, they later came to be seen more and more as shaitans (satans), and while there is no record of possession by demons in early Jewish history, that is the only type of possession reported by the authors of the Gospels.

We may assume that both the positive regard for possession and the frequency of the phenomenon increased again in the Christian world as a consequence of the experience of the Apostles on the day of Pentecost. From the writings of St. Paul we may infer that the effects of the Holy Spirit were well known during his time. (Consider, for instance, the admonition in the Epistle to the Ephesians: "Be not drunken with wine, wherein is riot, but be filled with the Spirit.") Ecstatic prophecy, nevertheless, was viewed with suspicion by the early Church, and when it was revived by Montanus in the second century, he and his followers were exterminated as heretics. The sayings of Montanus ring of the prophetic spirit of all times and places:

Man is like a lyre, and I [the Holy Spirit] play him like a plectrum. Man sleeps; I [the Holy Spirit] am awake.

The attitudes and interpretations the Church adopted with regard to the revival of possession in medieval witchcraft are too well known to call for more than a brief mention. Only with the Reformation did this phenomenon find a modest place in Christianity: in the early meetings of the Quakers in seventeenth-century England and, in present practice, as the religious core of minor sects such as the Pentecostals.

This historical digression is most relevant to the question of technique in the path of surrender for, if the "devil" is the misinterpretation of the "god" (because of our rigid assumptions and imperfect surrender), doesn't this make possession by the devil the unavoidable first step for one who shares this bias? In other words, in surrendering to his own nature, the individual may at first experience the emergence of unconscious intrusions of "devilish" nature, and only later come to "shake hands" with what, after all, was nothing other than his own energies, his constructive potential.

I am not thinking specifically of "devil-worship," though some historical forms of it may be related to this process, but of a more general principle: the conversion of "negative" into "positive" forces, or the recognition of a constructive power in what at first seems destructive. A typical instance of this is to be found in the shamanistic approach to helping spirits, which are often perceived at first as threatening, but which must be "tamed" in the overcoming of the shaman's nervous crisis.

Among the Angmagssalik Eskimos, what often takes the form of a shaman's spontaneous crisis is probably no different in nature (though perhaps in degree) from the crisis that the shaman is able to bring about in his function as a healer. Just as he has been able to come to terms with seemingly destructive forces (by giving in or riding with them), he is able to guide others on a similar journey. This entails a redirecting of the drives that are manifested in the form of mental or psychosomatic disease, and is essentially a process of giving such drives a channel of *expression:* dancing, imagery, drawing, dramatization, the emotionally expressive medium of gibberish (glossalalia). In being expressed, the "spirit" will have fulfilled its calling: once accepted, it will not need anymore to knock at the door of the individual's consciousness in the form of an ailment.

If we consider this situation in which religion, medicine, and art meet, we might well say that only in allowing himself to be *possessed by the spirit* (in dance, song, etc.) can the person *express himself*, and, consequently, create and become cured. Only in being taken over by a genie, can he become a genius.*

A particularly interesting instance of the transmutation of disease into constructive expression is afforded by the Zar cult of Iran, Ethiopia, Egypt, and Arabia, observable to this day. This is a form of healing practice in which the patient (afflicted by what we would regard as emotional or psychosomatic disturbances) *is regarded as possessed* from the outset, and in his being persuaded that in this possession lies the root of his sickness, he is also prompted to open up to the expression of the possessing entity. In the Zar healing ceremony the patient falls into a trance during which the intruding spirit in him can speak and make its demands clear. If satisfied, it agrees to leave the patient in peace.

The interpretation of disease as possession is far from being a rarity. Not only is it a common belief in the Middle East of today, but it was prevalent in Egyptian and Babylonian antiquity. We may regard the process that takes place in the Zar cult (or similar practices) as one of *surrogate* expression: under the special circumstances of the ceremony and, particularly, under the pretext of an alien spirit in his body, the patient may express *himself*, say what *he* wants, satisfy his postponed needs. But does not the *idea* of possession amount here to a powerful therapeutic technique, without which the cathartic process would have needed perhaps years on the psychoanalytic couch?

---

* The word "genius," which we now use to denote a certain type of excellence, derives from the notion of a possessing genie or jinn. To "have" genius once meant to have a helping spirit, a daimon.

The same interpretation is reported in other cultures (Greenland, Australia) as one of being swallowed by a monster and emerging out of it as a new man (cf. Jonah), or being taken to the underworld, torn apart and put together again, killed and resurrected:

> The first thing the disciple has to do is to go to a certain lonely spot, an abyss or a cave, and there, having taken a small stone, rub it on the top of a large one, the way of the sun. When they have done this for three days on end, they say, a spirit comes out from the rock. It turns its face toward the rising sun and asks what the disciple will. The disciple then dies in the most horrible torments, partly from fear, partly from overstrain; but he comes to life again, later in the day.[9]

There are special instances of the use of such personification in contemporary psychotherapy—notably Gestalt therapy and psychodrama—and in these we can see a type of psychological healing not different in essence from that of the shamanistic conversion of an "enemy" into a "helper." By confronting and even taking sides with the hitherto avoided aspects of his personality, the patient learns that these may be expressed in ways not detrimental to his life but, on the contrary, enriching. When this becomes possible, the devious mechanism at the root of his symptoms is no longer necessary.

The sudden flooding of the mind by unconscious (or, better, ego-alien) contents, which is characteristic of the kinds of spiritual practice under discussion, is not only most dramatic but also entails real dangers. The relationship between possession accompanied by visionary phenomena and psychosis can be seen at all levels. Not only do the prophet and the "God-intoxicated" frequently act like madmen, but a specific pathology seems to derive from the failure of the individual to deal with the avalanche of energies awakened by a practice of this type. Moreover, we may be justified in considering many cases of schizophrenia as an outcome of the spontaneous plunging of an immature person into the realm of that kind of experience, which, when properly assimilated, distinguishes the genius from the average man.

The shamanistic process, the cults of Egyptian and Greek Mysteries, the Sufi science of opening the lataif, the practice indirectly alluded to by Western and Taoistic texts on alchemy, all appear to deal with the domain of experience that has the potential of bringing the individual into harmonious contact with his unsuspected dormant powers or, alternately, of turning him into a puppet of forces that he cannot control. One of the reasons for the esoteric nature of many of the techniques employed in these various traditions lies in the dangers of misuse that are inherent in them. A dervish tale illustrates this point. It tells—such is the version of it in the *Arabian Nights*—of a fisherman who brought up a bottle from the ocean in his net. When he opened it a jinn came out and threatened to destroy him, but he managed to trick the jinn back into the bottle and throw it into the ocean. . . .

> Many years passed, until one day another fisherman, grandson of the first, cast his net in the same place, and brought up the self-same bottle.
>
> He placed the bottle upon the sand and was about to open it when a thought struck him. It was the piece of advice which had been passed down to him by his father, from *his* father.
>
> It was: "Man can use only what he has learned to use."
>
> And so it was that when the jinn, aroused from his slumbers by the movement of his metal prison, called through the brass: "Son of Adam, whoever you may be, open the stopper of this bottle and release me: for I am the Chief of the Jinns, who know the secrets of miraculous happenings," the young fisherman, remembering his ancestral adage, placed the bottle carefully in a cave and scaled the heights of a near-by cliff, seeking the cell of a wise man who lived there.
>
> He told the story to the wise man, who said: "Your adage is perfectly true: and you have to do this thing yourself, though you must know how to do it."

"But what do I have to do?" asked the youth.

"There is something, surely, that you feel you want to do?" said the other.

"What I want to do is to release the jinn, so that he can give me miraculous knowledge: or perhaps mountains of gold, and seas made from emeralds, and all the other things which jinns can bestow."

"It has not, of course, occurred to you," said the sage, "that the jinn might not give you these things when released; or that he may give them to you and then take them away because you have no means to guard them; quite apart from what might befall you if and when you did have such things, since 'Man can use only what he has learned to use.' "

"Then what should I do?"

"Seek from the jinn a sample of what he can offer. Seek a means of safeguarding that sample and testing it. Seek knowledge, not possessions, for possessions without knowledge are useless, and that is the cause of all our distractions."

Now, because he was alert and reflective, the young man worked out his plan on the way back to the cave where he had left the jinn.

He tapped on the bottle, and the jinn's voice answered, tinny through the metal, but still terrible: "In the name of Solomon the Mighty, upon whom be peace, release me, son of Adam!"

"I don't believe that you are who you say and that you have the powers which you claim," answered the youth.

"Don't believe me! Do you not know that I am incapable of telling a lie?" the jinn roared back.

"No, I do not," said the fisherman.

"Then how can I convince you?"

"By giving me a demonstration. Can you exercise any powers through the wall of the bottle?"

"Yes," admitted the jinn, "but I cannot release myself through these powers."

"Very well, then: give me the ability to know the truth of the problem which is on my mind."

Instantly, as the jinn exercised his strange craft, the fisherman became aware of the source of the adage handed down by his grandfather. He saw, too, the whole scene of the release of the jinn from the bottle; and he also saw how he could convey to others how to gain such capacities from the jinn. But he also realized that there was no more that he could do. And so the fisherman picked up the bottle and, like his grandfather, cast it into the ocean.

And he spent the rest of his life not as a fisherman but as a man who tried to explain to others the perils of "Man trying to use what he has not learned to use."

But, since few people ever came across jinns in bottles, and there was no wise man to prompt them in any case, the successors of the fisherman garbled what they called his "teachings," and mimed his descriptions. In due course they became a religion, with brazen bottles from which they sometimes drank housed in costly and well-adorned temples. And, because they respected the behaviour of this fisherman, they strove to emulate his actions and his deportment in every way.

The bottle, now many centuries later, remains the holy symbol and mystery for these people. They try to love each other only because they love this fisherman; and in the place where he settled and built a humble shack they deck themselves with finery and move in elaborate rituals.

Unknown to them, the disciples of the wise man still live; the descendants of the fisherman are unknown. The brass bottle lies at the bottom of the sea with the jinn slumbering within.[10]

The danger of psychosis that besets the legendary sorcerer's apprentice is today a matter of great interest, because we are beginning to see that not only is psychosis the outcome of a failure of the ego (to deal with the unconscious) but also a state of potentialities greater than those of the normal states. Julian Silverman has remarked on how a shaman undergoes, as part of his initiation process, something that we would diagnose as a psychotic state.[11] He is not hospitalized for it and "treated," but, quite to the contrary, his state is respected and allowed to follow its natural course. The consequent question is then: are not some of the syndromes that we treat as schizophrenic, tumultuous, and even cataclysmic, stages of development that we are, for lack of trust, interrupting instead of allowing them to take a positive course?

A new approach to psychosis, now gaining adherents, is more respectful than the traditional, and we may therefore hope that definitive answers to the question are not too far away.* At any rate, from the facts known to us now, it may be said that practices in surrender of control (such as mediumship) *may* lead to psychotic states and that temporary states akin to psychosis are part of the inner journey of *some* shamans, mystics, and artists.

Aside from the esoteric character of some practices, there are a number of factors that make it difficult to write on techniques pertaining to the revelatory dimension of meditation. One such factor relates to the nature of the defining attitude. Because of its openness to the promptings from one's deeper nature, and its attunement to one's inner voices, the way may be expected to be a highly *individual* one. Indeed, if we seek analogies for the shamanistic way in the modern world, the closest might be found in the life of some artists, whose endeavor has been to follow their "calling" or vocation. Their attunement to themselves (or, if we prefer, to what wanted expression through them) cannot in general be divorced from their process of expression, so that their art is at the same time a result and a discipline. When the Greeks spoke of the poet as one possessed by the Muses, they were not merely indulging in a metaphor. For many, the visionary or clairaudient experience was as true as that which Socrates reported in speaking of his daimon, and this has continued to be true among a number of artists in our own tradition.

Dante writes: "I am one who when Love inspires me, takes

* An international conference on the value of psychotic experiences was held at Esalen Institute in 1968, and a forthcoming book edited by J. Silverman will present a summary of the more important contributions.

note; and I go on setting it forth after the fashion which Love dictates within me." In Whitman we read:

> Oh, I am sure they come from Thee, the urge, the order, the unconquerable will, the potent, felt, interior command, stronger than words. A message from the heavens, whispering to me ever in my sleep.

They are both speaking of the true experience of *inspiration*, which most people today have come to regard as little more than a figure of speech. Such experiences do not differ in essence from that which Alfred de Musset describes in the following terms: ". . . it is not work. It is merely listening. It is as if some unknown person were speaking in your ear."

Another factor that makes description of techniques of meditation difficult is that the effectivness of any technique seems to depend on an extra-technical factor of "personal contagion."

The infectious nature of possession by devils throughout history is well established, and it is impressive to read documents such as those of the epidemic of Loudun, showing how even apparently sane priests sent to perform exorcisms became affected by the prevalent state.[12]

What is true with regard to unwanted devil possession is apparently as true with regard to states that are welcomed and cultivated. Among many peoples, trance is a collective phenomenon in which the state of the more experienced is believed to facilitate that of the novices. The Kung Bushmen of the Kalahari Desert, for instance, understand the possessing entity not as a spirit but as an energy* (also called a "medicine") originally given to man by God and now maintained by direct *transmission* from man to man. According to Dr. R. Lee, who has studied the trance dances, the practicing curers spend much of their time implanting "medicine" into the bodies of their trainees.[13]

---

* Interestingly, not unlike the Taoist elizir or the Power of Kundalini Yoga, this is a "medicine" that lies in the pit of the stomach and, when heated up, rises in the form of vapors through the spinal column.

That the direct transmission of a spiritual energy, or the possibility for a divinely inspired individual to bring another into contact with his seemingly supernatural source of inspiration, is well recognized in the different mystical traditions can be seen in stereotyped expressions that have lost their original significance, such as the notion of "blessing," or the Christian formula of insufflation during baptism, "Receive ye the Holy Spirit." In other instances, however, it is a matter of a non-verbal process by which a spiritual master may actually initiate a disciple to a new domain of experience. The following passage of the Sufi Master Ibn' Arabi —known as a "disciple of Khidr"—tells of his own initiation to the state of communion with the cosmic entity that the Sufis equate with the Holy Spirit, with the Angel Gabriel, and with the historical Elijah:

This consocation with Khidr was experienced by one of our *shaikhs*, the *shaikh* 'Ali ibn 'Abdillah ibn Jami, who was one of the disciples of 'Ali al-Mutawakkil and of Abu Abdillah Qadib Alban. He lived in a garden he owned in the outskirts of Mosul. There Khidr had invested him with the mantle in the presence of Qadib Alban. And it was in that very spot, in the garden where Khidr had invested him with it that the *shaikh* invested me with it in turn, observing the same ceremonial as Khidr himself had observed in conferring the investiture upon him. I had already received this investiture, but more indirectly, at the hands of my friend Taqiuddin ibn Abdirrahman, who himself had received it at the hands of Sadruddin, *shaikh* of *shaikhs* in Egypt, whose grandfather had received it from Khidr. It was then that I began to speak of the investiture with the mantle and to confer it upon cerain persons, because I discovered how much importance Khidr attached to this rite. Previously I had not spoken of the mantle which is now well known. This mantle is for us indeed a symbol of confraternity, a sign that we share in the same spiritual culture, in the practice of the same *ethos*. It has become customary among the masters of mysticism that when they discern some deficiency in one of their disciples, the *shaikh* identifies himself mentally with the state of perfection he wishes to communicate. When he has effected this identification, he takes off the mantle he is wearing at the moment of achieving this spiritual state, and puts it on the disciple whose spiritual state he wishes to make perfect. In this way the *shaikh* communicates to the disciple the spiritual state he has produced in himself, and the same perfection is achieved in the disciple's state. Such is the rite of investiture, well known among us; it was communicated to us by the most experienced, among our *shaikhs*.[14]

For each type of concentrative meditation, one is likely to find a corresponding type of expressive meditation. Meditation on externally given visual images has its correspondence, among the expressive techniques, in the contemplation of spontaneously arising imagery; meditation on a verbal formula crystallizing a definite state of mind (such as the koan) has in it the formulation of the hitherto unformulated state of the meditator. To traditionally stereotyped dance forms will correspond a form of dancing in which the individual aims at becoming transparent to the music and letting the dance, so to speak, do itself.*

Even in the domain of breathing we can contrast the two approaches. On the one hand, we find formalized exercises like pranayama,† which involve control of the breath and the surrender of spontaneous preference in favor of a pre-established rhythm; on the other hand, we have a practice that involves the relinquishing of control and a surrender of preference in favor of a spontaneity in the breathing process that originates in a level deeper than that of conscious choice. Even in this simple psychophysiological sphere we thus find a correspondence between the two approaches, a confluence that religions have described as the doing of God's will: the way of the Law, given from without, and that of Revelation, from within; the unfolding of the Divine seed planted in man's innermost nature.

---

* There are, however, exceptions: some trance dances (like the Balinese) are stereotyped. In the highly structured movements of Tai Chi Chuan, on the other hand, the aim is spontaneity and the flow of *chi* is an energy conceived in terms similar to those reported by the Bushmen.
† The fourth limb of Astanga Yoga or Raja Yoga.

The breathing exercise may seem, from such a written description, easy to carry out and perhaps trivial. We may tend to believe that "breathing naturally" is the most simple thing to do and that we are already doing it. In fact we *are*, but *only when we are not aware* of breathing. While we go about our ordinary activities, our breathing center—the animal within us—directs our respiratory movements with great wisdom according to the needs of our organism. As soon as "we" notice our breathing, however, "we" cannot hold back from interfering. Our conscious ego is a great manipulator that only through special training can learn to be *merely* aware. The exercise in spontaneous conscious breathing, therefore, is that of becoming a permissive observer, a non-intruding witness of nature—and in that, it is a practice in surrender and in action-in-inaction. This exercise, which is of great importance in the Buddhistic tradition, may be regarded as the simplest conceivable practice in naturalness and the first step toward disciplines in naturalness of movement (such as Zen archery or painting) and in mind-at-large.[15]

The attitude we have described above, which can be characterized as one of letting a process happen and "being breathed by one's breath," becomes, in the domain of visual representation, one of letting imagery unfold without conscious interference. Just as in the case of breathing, we would be wrong in assuming that this is something that we already do in our ordinary daydreaming. Only in *unconscious* daydreaming or in nocturnal dreaming—when "we" are not present—do we let go of control in our imaginary activity, and even then to a moderate degree.

True freedom of the mind is an attitude that many poets and painters have intentionally cultivated. It has led them to feel that their work was creating itself through them. In the domain of pure imagery, however, the situation is simplified by the absence of any technical issue such as that implied by the holding of pencil and brush.

The practice of unstructured contemplation of imagery is so widespread that it encompasses such different examples as the "hunting for visions" of American Indians and the astral scrying of magicians. Under the name of "active imagination," it holds a prominent place in Jungian psychology,[16] and under that of "guided daydream," it is a different version of the practice recently discovered independently by Desoille.[17] Various psychotherapeutic schools today (such as Gestalt therapy and psychosynthesis) make use of the inner-directed display of visual fantasy as occasion suggests and in the context of their characteristic styles. Without forgetting that progress in the ability to let go of voluntary manipulation—in fantasy as well as in breathing—is more a matter of practice and self-observation than of sophisticated techniques, it is useful to keep in mind certain conditions, such as the necessity of sustained, concentrated attention to the unfolding of imagery. Muscular relaxation may also facilitate the practice, and, as with any form of training extending over time, regularity is important to success. With persistent practice, even persons who are not good visualizers are likely to notice a gradual shift in the quality of their imagination. While not unlike habitual daydreams at first, their productions will tend to resemble more and more those of the natural dream in their spontaneity and apparently irrational quality. Finally, as this level is also left behind, fantasies of a mythical quality, reflecting the archetypal level of the mind, become more prominent.

Techniques of letting go of control in the domain of fantasy are by no means the only ones that have found their way into psychotherapy. Indeed, most of psychotherapy today consists of variations upon the underlying motif of liberation of man's organismic tendencies from the prison of his conditioning.

The basic technique of psychoanalysis—"free association"—is the perfect reflection, at the conceptual level, of the practice of non-interfering observation that we encountered in the breathing exercise described earlier. The specific contribution of psychoanalysis to the attainment of this freedom is in the participation of the second person who witnesses the process: the activity known as "analysis of resistances." For, just as it may take devoted attention to discover that our "natural" breathing is not natural and our "spontaneous" fantasies are controlled, it may be necessary for us to develop a deeper insight in order to understand that our "free association" is unfree. According to Sandor Ferenczi, who may be called one of the fathers of the psychoanalytic technique, when a person attains the ability to free-associate, his analysis may be deemed completed. From this point of view, the technique of psychoanalysis is, like techniques of meditation in general, both a path and a goal.

A similar strategy of de-structuring individual behavior in order to facilitate the emergence of inner structure or style represents the foundation of several schools of group psychotherapy, from group psychoanalysis to encounter. The basic rule in all of these is self-expression, and the goal that of letting self-identity emerge from the superimposed socially patterned behavior that we have come to regard as "self."

One more instance of the way of expression and liberation in the province of psychotherapy is to be found in certain ways of employing psychoactive drugs. As with other techniques, the use of drugs to induce trance states appears to be of great antiquity and is generally found in association with shamanistic practice. The association of Dionysian rites with wine is well known, and it appears from various descriptions that the trance of the sybil at the Delphic Oracle was aided by her inhalation of the vapors of the chasm and of the fumes of laurel. There are indications, too, that some drug was employed at the Mysteries of Eleusis. "I have tasted, I have drunk the *cyceon*," says an oft-quoted statement by the Mystai (initiates).

Just as drugs have been traditionally employed as catalysts to achieve self-expressive and prophetic attitudes, so their most promising place in contemporary psychotherapy seems to be in connection with the techniques aiming at unfolding suppressed spontaneity. For instance:

1. The use of intravenous amphetamines or MDA in order to elicit recall of repressed traumatic memories and feelings.

2. The use of harmaline or ibogaine as facilitators of the guided fantasy or similar practices and, in general, as bridges to the archetypal domain.[18]

3. The use of LSD and related drugs to induce a state of temporary unlearning of perceptual or social stereotypes, in which the individual may become receptive to his unconditioned or true needs and reactions.[19]

It is no wonder that several forms of practice in letting go to our deeper propensities are now to be found in the field of psychotherapy, for psychotherapy as a whole (as most frequently conceived today) aims at liberating the individual from what hinders from within his expression or realization.[20]

As to the relationship between art and therapy as ways of expression and liberation, it may be said that art centers in the issue of expression, and therapy in that of removing the blocks to expression, but any sharp boundary between the two processes can only be artificial. The shaman was at the same time an artist and a healer, and today we seem to be entering a stage of decompartmentalization of disciplines through which we can understand their original unity. More specifically, art-education disciplines are becoming therapies, and therapy is seen as both an art (rather than a medical technique independent of the inner states of the "patient") and a means of liberating the artist in the patient.

Another technique that deserves special attention is the one that has attracted many adherents all over the Western world today as a consequence of the influence of the Indonesian Bapak Subuh. The main practice carried out in different branches of Subud is called *latihan* and consists, precisely, in a surrender of control. The words that are generally used at the beginning of a session define the practice as a specific form of isvara-pranidhana*: "Let us surrender to the will of God." The specificity of the context lies in the fact that it is carried out in groups of either men or

* See p. 63.

women, and that a restriction is placed on the possible impulse to touch or address other persons in the group.

The phenomena typical of the latihan are mostly those already described: ecstatic experiences, visionary experiences in the form of hallucinations or eidetic imagery, possession or manifestations related to possession, such as automatic movements, glossolalia, inspired singing, spontaneously unfolding rituals. Otherwise the latihan may take the form of a serene receptive state akin to that in Za-Zen, or a tranquil attunement to what the individual perceives as God's will. Alternatively, it may be an experience of purification through the awareness of lack of attunement, either in that very moment or, more generally, in the individual's ordinary life.

According to Idries Shah, the latihan is a Sufi exercise not to be recommended as a single practice divorced from its original context or expert supervision.[21] Perhaps this is a statement valid for all the exercises mentioned, because they can represent a way both out of or into mental disease. They are ways of liberation through chaos, ways to consciousness via the unconscious, and, as Jung has pointed out about deep psychotherapy, there is the danger of remaining paralyzed in the depths and not returning.

The *latihan* is no exception to the expressive way in general, in that it may be an avenue to psychotic experience. Even psychoanalysis can be such an avenue, and it is not uncommon for psychotic experiences, elicited by the analytic process, to be the prelude to the definitive cure. However, the *latihan* (like the ingestion of drugs) may not only be a particularly ample gateway to the other side of the mind, but call for the complement of highly skilled guidance.

What I am saying of techniques of surrendering control in general is particularly true, I believe, of a technique that has received little attention in professional circles but whose potential danger might well be turned into usefulness. This is automatic writing.

Automatic writing is a phenomenon not known to most persons, and yet it is susceptible of being experienced by many (and perhaps most). It is done by holding a pencil over a sheet of paper without attempting to write, but only waiting for an involuntary movement to develop. If the experiment is engaged in with some persistence, it is very likely that the subject will find that his hand moves by itself, "as if guided by an invisible power." This may lead, at first, to illegible scribbling, but in the course of time it will take the shape of writing that can be understood. The experience is most likely to be successful when a question is posed by the subject, either aloud or mentally, and when this question is one whose answer deeply concerns him. Then the writing will have relevance to the question, and it is likely to impress the subject as an answer not formulated by himself. Moreover, as in the phenomenon of possession or in some deliberately induced hypnotic states, the person who writes sometimes does not know the content of his writing at all until a statement is completed.*

After persistent practice in automatic writing, however, texts dealing with personal matters often tend to be replaced by more impersonal or transpersonal ones, generally associated with the emergence of definite answering personalities (regardless of whether these are interpreted or not as "spirits" by the subject). When this occurs, it can be said that automatic writing has led to a more complete expression of the possession syndrome, with the dangers or the blessings, whichever may be the case.

I want to describe in some detail two instances of an inner saga triggered by automatic writing. Both cases are what may be called *monumenta psychologica* and show the organic interrelationships among a number of features of the expressive way and its states.

* The interested reader may find useful technical information on the procedure in a book by Dr. A. Mühl,[22] who employed it in a psychotherapeutic context. As Dr. William Alanson White puts it in his introduction to the work, she had employed automatic writing "for discovering what was going on in the mind of her patients which was inaccessible to ordinary questioning."

The first case is that of Ludwig Staudenmeier, a professor of experimental chemistry, who in 1910 published a long essay entitled "Die Magie als experimentelle Naturwissenschaft" (Magic as an Experimental Science).[23] He was a methodical person with a critical mind, who started experimenting with automatic writing out of scientific curiosity. Once that Pandora box of his mind was opened, his life became a struggle to master the forces he had unleashed in his own psyche.

Staudenmeier was persuaded by a friend to try automatic writing. After several failures, his friend encouraged him to go on, until finally his pencil described "the strangest loops and curlicues." Later, and in spite of his skepticism, letters began to form and answers to the questions he was formulating. Though different spirits claimed to be involved in the writing, Staudenmeier doubted this, for he realized that his own thoughts were involved in the answers. "Nevertheless," he wrote, "I absolutely had the impression of having to do with a being utterly alien to me. At first I could tell in advance what was going to be written, and from this there developed in time an anticipated 'inner' hearing of the message; . . . as the spiritualists say, I had become an 'auditory medium.' "[24]

Some of the voices that Staudenmeier described are similar to those reported by most mediums as well as schizophrenics with auditory delusions:

> If the end the inner voice . . . made itself heard too often and without sufficient reason, and also against my will; a number of times it was bad, subtly mocking, vexatious, and irritable. For whole days at a time this insufferable struggle continued entirely against my will.

> Often the statements of these so-called beings proved to be fabrications. Opposite the house where I live a strange tenant was just moving in. By way of test I asked my spirits his name. Without hesitation I received the reply: Hauptmann von Müller. It later proved that the information was completely false. When in such a case I afterward reproached them gently, I often elicited this

sincere reply: "It is because we cannot do otherwise, we are obliged to lie, we are evil spirits, you must not take it amiss!" If I then became rude they followed suit.

"Go to blazes, you fool! You are always worrying us! You ought not to have summoned us! Now we are always obliged to stay near you!" When I used stronger language it was exactly as if I had hurled insults at a wall or a forest: the more one utters the more the echo sends back. For a time the slightest unguarded thought that passed through my mind produced an outburst from the inner voices.[25]

In the course of time, some of the voices became highly individualized and endowed with some characteristics more related to possession than to hallucination. The three most persistent of these he called "my highness," "the child," and "Roundhead." Here are some of Staudenmeier's descriptions of the first two:

Later there were manifested in a similar manner personifications of princely or ruling individuals, such as the German Emperor, and furthermore of deceased persons such as Napoleon the First. At the same time a characteristic feeling of loftiness took possession of me; I became the lord and master of a great people, my chest swelled and broadened almost without any action on my part, my attitude became extremely energetic and military, a proof that the said personification was then exercising an important influence. For example, I heard the inner voice say to me majestically: "I am the German Emperor." After some time I grew tired, other conceptions made themselves strongly felt and my attitude once more relaxed. Thanks to the number of personalities of high rank who made their appearance to me, the idea of grandeur and nobility gradually developed. My highness is possessed by a great desire to be a distinguished personality, even a princely or governing personality, or at least—this is how I explain after the event—to see and imitate these personalities. My highness takes great interest in military spectacles, fashionable life, distinguished bearing, good living with abundant choice beverages, order and elegance within the house, fine clothing, an upright military carriage, gymnastics, hunting and other sports, and seeks accordingly to influence my mode of life by advice, exhortations, orders and threats. On the other hand, my highness is averse to children, common things, jesting and gaiety, evidently because he knows princely persons almost exclusively by their ceremonial attitude in public or by illustrations. He particularly detests illustrated journals of satirical caricatures, total abstainers, etc. I am, moreover, somewhat too small for him.

Another important role is played by the "child" personification: "I am a child. You are the father. You must play with me." Then childish verses are hummed. "The little wheel goes thud, thud, thud," "Comes a little flying bird." Wonderfully tender childishness, and artless ways such as no real child would show in so marked and touching a manner. In moments of good humour I am called Putzi, or else he says simply, "My dear Zi." When walking in town I must stop at the toy-shop windows, make a detailed inspection, buy myself toys, watch the children playing, romp on the ground, and dance in a ring as children do, thus consistently behaving with an entire absence of loftiness. If on the request of "the child" or "the children" (at times there occurred a division into several kindred personalities), I happen to pause in a shop and look over the toy counter, this personification bubbles over with joy and in a childish voice cries out ecstatically: "Oh, how lovely! It's really heavenly!"

Since the "child" personification has acquired a greater influence over me, not only has my interest in childish ways, toys, and even shops increased, but also my search for childish satisfactions and the innocent joys of the heart, a fact which acts upon the organism, rejuvenating and refreshing it, and driving away many of the cares of the grown man, accustomed more and more to use his intelligence. In the same way a number of other personifications also have a beneficial effect upon me. For example, my interest in art and understanding of artistic things have increased considerably. Particularly remarkable and characteristic of the profound division which takes place in me is the following fact: that whereas my interest in art was formerly very slight, especially as regards that of antiquity and the Middle Ages, certain of my personifications are passionately interested in these latter and have continually impelled me to devote attention to them."[26]

Staudenmeier's experiments led him to a number of discoveries that I will not detail in this context—in spite of their being more extraordinary than mere possession experiences. As for the self-perfecting quest into which he stumbled unwillingly, he apparently failed to reach his goal. At least we know that two and one-half years before his death, at the age of sixty-six, he wrote in a postcard to a friend: "I am continuing with my work with desperate energy, but it is very slow and difficult. Although all four of the recalcitrant centers have received ample blows in their personifications partly from one another and partly from me, they fall back again and again into their old errors so that it really takes the patience of a lamb to persevere."[27]

The second case of a life profoundly affected by automatic writing is that of another scientist whose pursuit of knowledge became a pursuit of wisdom and a spiritual quest. The difference from Staudenmeier is that in this instance we can speak of a completed development, in the same sense that, in shamanism, the initiate not only plunges into seeming madness but emerges from it "reborn" before undertaking his work.

I am speaking of Emanuel Swedenborg, who may be called a modern shaman, not only because of the nature of his journey, his visionary experiences, and the multiplicity of his interests and gifts, but because his whole spiritual adventure unfolded from his following the bent of his inner nature.

Swedenborg, mineralogist, physicist, biologist, philosopher, and adviser to the Swedish government in the early eighteenth century, has been one of the few men of encompassing genius in the history of Europe. William Blake, Goethe, Heine, Balzac, Emerson, Henry James, the Brownings, and many other writers have praised him or acknowledged a debt to his ideas, while his scientific theories foreshadowed what dozens of specialists were to confirm in the following years. He was the first, for instance, to formulate the idea of cerebral localizations and to describe the functions of the brain cortex. Also, a hundred years before the neuronal structure of the brain cortex had been observed, he attributed the primary functions of nervous control to little oval particles in the gray matter. Arrhenius, in an introduction to the cosmological section of Swedenborg's *Prodromus Principiorum Rerum Naturalium*, concluded:

> If we briefly summarize the ideas which were first given expression by Swedenborg, and afterwards, though usually in a much modified form—consciously or unconsciously—taken up by other authors in cosmology, we find them to be:
>
> The planets of our solar system originate from the solar matter—taken up by Buffon, Kant, Laplace, and others.
>
> The earth and the other planets have gradually removed themselves from the sun and received a gradually lengthened time of revolution, a view again expressed by G. H. Darwin.
>
> The suns are arranged around the Milky Way, taken up by Wright, Kant, and Lambert.
>
> There are still greater systems in which the milky ways are arranged, taken up by Lambert.[28]

Swedenborg's early stage of spiritual development may be seen as that of a gnani-yogin. He was at first a scientist who turned his attention more and more to the basic questions of science (such as the nature of matter, or the mind-body problem) until, at the age of forty-two, he established a great synthesis of the knowledge of his time in the three big volumes of his *Opera Philosophica et Mineralia*. Driven through this work to consider the nexus between the infinite and the finite, eternity and time, he produced next a book entitled *Of The Infinite*. In the second part of this book, far from the a-religious stance that was characteristic of his early career, he proposed that the true divinity in man is an acknowledgment of the existence of God, "and the sense of delight in the love of God." His interest now turned to the "science of the soul," to complete which, he said, "all the sciences are required that the world has ever eliminated or developed." His reflections on this matter constitute the content of two volumes that he completed at the age of fifty-one and that bear the title *The Economy of The Animal Kingdom.* (This is a gross mistranslation from his Latin original; "animal" here stands for his word *anima*—"soul." The title should be "The Organization of the Soul's Kingdom," that is, the body).

It was apparently during this time that Swedenborg had the first clear-cut indications of an order of experience other than that with which he was familiar. He became very interested in his dreams, of which he started to keep a journal, and he discovered an ability to cut off his sense impressions when he wanted to think intensely. Perhaps of greater importance is his statement that when men of science who have the power of synthesizing, "after a long course of reasoning make a discovery of the truth, straightaway there is a certain cheering light, a joyful confirmatory brightness, that plays round the sphere of their mind; a kind of mysterious radiation—I know not whence it proceeds—that darts through some secret temple of the brain." The following quotation from later writing probably refers to the same experience, or to the development of it in subsequent years:

> . . . a flame of diverse sizes and with a diversity of color and splendor has often been seen by me. Thus while I was writing a certain little work hardly a day passed by for several months in which a flame was not seen by me as vividly as the flame of a household hearth; at the time this was a sign of approbation, and this happened before spirits began to speak with me viva voce.[29]

Experiences of this type, culminating in a vision of Christ, profoundly changed Swedenborg and resulted in a book entitled *Of The Worship and Love of God.* After this, not even his writing would be his own: his next eight volumes were, as he said, *inspired:* "Nay have I written entire pages, and the spirits did

not dictate the words, but absolutely guided my hands, so
that it may [be assumed to be]* they who were doing the writing."

Signe Toksvig, author of an appreciative biography of Swedenborg, writes of *The Word Explained:* "There probably never
has been anything written so overpoweringly alien to normal interest as these Biblical commentaries by Swedenborg, nor anything more foreign to the results of modern Biblical research.
Neither has anything served so much to conceal the true great-
ness of the man. No one who chances to meet him first in these
earnest crossword puzzles can be blamed for turning quickly
away."

There are indications that some of the contents of the exegesis
were repulsive to his own mind. Yet Swedenborg respected it
all as *revelation*, for "these words were written by my hand,
and dictated by Isaac, the father of the Jews. . . ." Other parts
were written by Jacob, by Abraham, by Moses, or by "the
Messiah himself through Abraham."

But, according to Toksvig, Swedenborg early began to lose
faith in the declared identities of the spirits, and it is evident
that he was worried by their claim that "they were doing the
dictation." At the end, he came to believe that the spirits claiming
to be Biblical patriarchs were truly impostors. Yet his own writing continued,† now inspired by more trustworthy entities. In a
diary entry of this period he stated that he did not accept any
"representation, vision or discourse" from spirit or angel without
reflection on them "as to what thence was truthful and good."
Since "truthful" and "good" were to him from the Lord, he
could say that he had been instructed "by no spirit or by any
angel but by the Lord alone from whom is all truth and good."

This is an important statement. No longer does Swedenborg

---

* The original source is unclear at this point.
† The eight volumes of *Arcana Coelestia*, written during this period, were
a new attempt to explain the inner meaning of Genesis and Exodus.

equate the fruit of inspiration with truth, nor does he leave this decision to reason alone. The ability to *discriminate* truth, like the confirmatory light experienced during his writing in earlier years, is in itself a gift of intuition. *He* could only say, "*I know.*" During the later decades of his life he produced his most profound works, in which he *brought together* his highly uncommon inspiration with his ordering, critical mind. Through the years his discrimination became more subtle, we may surmise, so that he could be enriched by messages beyond his reasoning faculties and still be a creator and master of his world picture. Thus, when a friend asked him how many he had succeeded in persuading of the truth of his doctrines, he could say, after reflection, that he thought he had "about fifty in this world and about the same number in the other."[30]

I have given what might seem inordinate attention to these two illustrations of automatic writing because of their bearing on much of what I have touched upon in this chapter. Both Staudenmeier and Swedenborg are instances of visionaries and men who experienced possession states; both illustrate the unleashing of unsuspected forces within their own psyches; both raise the question as to the boundaries between mysticism and schizophrenia; and both evidence what we regard as supernatural or "psychic" abilities.*

Beyond all this, these two lives illustrate another more fundamental feature of the dimension of spontaneity that we have been discussing: they were solitaries who learned everything from their own experience and inspiration. In contrast to individuals who have trodden the way of meditation on symbolic forms or the way of emptiness, they are eminently free from tradition, finding guidance only within themselves. And, we may add, only individual instances can properly illustrate the way of

---

* Staudenmeier could cause action at a distance and was able to impress an image on a photographic plate; Swedenborg was well known for feats of clairvoyance that have become historical.

expression. *What* is expressed may be in the final analysis the same for each enlightened prophet, all the disciples of Melchizedek being prompted by a selfsame inner spirit. And yet their ways are unique, and their process of realization directed by their peculiar background and situation. Their way is essentially *the way of vocation*, that of listening to their inner voice, and their path one of gradual approximation. Had Swedenborg not taken down the messages of the spirit-world imposters, would he have been able to know them for what they were, and receive the more refined messages of later years?*

The way of forms is based upon the predication: "Here is a truth: assimilate it; make it yours." The way of expression starts out from the opposite prospect: "The truth lies within you, and you can find it only by forgetting the ready-made answers."

These are two attitudes that bear upon life in general, not merely upon the sphere of meditation. An extension of the assimilative and unitive approach is an attitude of respect for established forms and feelings of reverence for crystallized wisdom. The formalist is typically pious. The corresponding extension of the way of expression to life at large is that self-assurance and disrespect for established forms which is frequently part of the personality of a genius and has given rise to the stereotype of the artist as a rebellious man. By questioning established knowledge those who have followed the way of expression have been able to contact—to a greater or lesser extent—the source of all answers without intermediaries, and thus have given new words, sounds, shapes to the eternal truth.

The same two attitudes may be seen in education, where the formalistic declares: "I have a truth. Listen!"; and the permissive, trusting a natural development within the individual, holds

---

* It is interesting to note that the phenomenon of intrusion is commonplace in spiritualistic circles. A remarkable instance of it may be found in William Yeats's work, "A Vision," completed after years of automatic writing frequently interrupted by "false teachers."

that the child can be nourished but cannot be guided without risk of interference or conditioning.

These attitudes may be found again in ethics, as a trust in absolutes, principles, and laws on the one hand, and a trust in free choice and responsibility on the other. In politics, they take the extreme forms of theocracy and democracy; in cultural styles, those of traditionalism and individualism, past-orientation and present-orientation.

In all these spheres today we seem to be passing from a state of formalism to one of relinquishing forms and seeking inner orientation. Our culture seems to be at a point of transition where the old forms are dying and people do not want new ones but seek to grasp the meaning that the older traditions have failed to express through excessive repetition.

Humanity is increasingly aware of the prison it has built for itself, and individuals want to be freed from what they are made to swallow whole by their environment. Because of this, man's metaphysical drive is leading him in the direction of expression, liberation, revelation from within.

5 / For a Theory of Meditation:
An Update

I had just come to California in the mid-1960s when I first started to conceptualize in regard to the domain of meditation, and I was only a beginning apprentice to whom heaven had granted some peak experiences. Then, as today, California was a melting pot of many traditions, and so I had the opportunity there of being exposed to various approaches—mainly Gestalt and psychedelic therapies, ZaZen, a form of Kundalini Yoga, and Charlotte Selver's "sensory awareness."

Then one day Joe Kamiya (now widely known because of his research on brain-wave control through biofeedback) invited me to the Langley Porter Neuropsychiatric Institute to give a talk on the psychology of meditation. To prepare for it, I collected what books on the subject I could find in print and was impressed with what different definitions and forms of meditation were proposed in them. Some spoke of meditation as always meditation *on* something—for instance, meditation on a concept, passage of scripture, or, more generally, an object; others (mostly those schooled

Adapted from a talk given at the Frankfurt Museum of Natural History under sponsorship of Frankfurter Ring.

in the Zen tradition) insisted on meditation being everything but meditation on something: meditation must *not* have an object.

The differences in definition could be multiplied, and it seemed that before one might propose a more encompassing definition or description of meditation, one would need first of all to stand before the whole meditation domain. I didn't deem it reasonable to restrict the term *meditation* to a specific part of the total field; there were enough points of similarity between different forms of meditation to conceive of them as near or distant points in a single domain. I developed a tri-polar graph, which I elaborated upon in 1970 when Dr. Ornstein invited me to coauthor a book on the subject.

In that book, *On the Psychology of Meditation*, I pointed out the distinction between one kind of meditation, which I there called "the negative way" (epitomized in the well-known Sanskrit dictum *neti neti*, "not this, not that," and involving a gesture of disidentifying with the objects of though or perception), with two contrasting groups and styles of meditation. One of these styles I called "concentrative meditation," in which the meditator focuses on a chosen object; we might say that we tell our mind what to do and we discipline it. The other style might be regarded as a discipline of undiscipline (in the sense of letting the mind go), a discipline of surrender. The contrast between concentrative meditation and the kind of meditation consisting in letting-go is one that I characterized through the labels "Apollonian" and "Dionysian." It seems to me that these concepts apply to the realm of spiritual endeavor even more appropriately than to styles of art and of culture.

On the Psychology of Meditation was published over fifteen years ago, and the main criticism that it has received has come from people schooled in the Buddhist tradition, for in Buddhism there is no explicit recognition of the "Dionysian" division of meditation. I have also called this type of meditation "the expressive way."

The traditional classification of meditation within the Buddhist tradition speaks of two kinds of practice: *samatha*, which consists of the calming of the mind; and *vipassana*, which consists of looking keenly at the state and content of the mind. Yet even though these are the *outspoken* goals of most Buddhist meditation, there is in the background of both an important component of letting-go. In Zen tradition, for instance, there is a great emphasis on spontaneity and on expression of the meditative state in life and art. Also in ZaZen itself the meditation process is an invitation not only to a quieting of the mind but to a non-obstructed state. Furthermore, surrender is usually facilitated by the practice of refuge to the Buddha, the *Dharma*, and the *Sangha* before practice sessions, and, as is well known to practioners and instructors in various nonexpressive techniques (from *anapana sati* to Taoist meditation), the practice of doing nothing evokes many spontaneous experiences that constitute the perceptual and subtle physical phenomena of control relinquishment.

There is a difference between the Buddhist tradition and others in this respect: in Buddhism, paying attention to these phenomena is not recommended—mostly as a safeguard against getting attached to them. To counteract the fascination they may arouse, the meditator is invited to look upon them as illusion and not be distracted from the goal of relinquishing all thought. This is understandable as a strategy in Zen, because it is the self-emptying and equanimity involved in this path that are the very source from which these visions arise. Yet we also find spiritual traditions that recommend the opposite strategy: one of honoring these visions as godlike and seeking guidance from them; even seeking guidance from within as to how to meditate, so that meditation is not something done according to this or that formula but is something like the "way of the fish" that monitors its direction as it moves along.

What I myself found imperfect about this tri-polar classification of meditation was that it did not distinguish very well between *vipassana*—the practice of pure mindfulness—and the practice of meditation on a fixed object. Because of this eventually I changed my meditation map into a fourfold one. More precisely, I thought it would be desirable to map meditation according to two *bipolar* dimensions—that is, two dimensions, each of which entails two extremes. The first of these I have called the stop/go dimension, for it is one that goes from not-doing to letting-go and has to do with the conative sphere—that is, with that of doing, in its wider sense comprising mental as well as physical activity. "Not-doing" and "letting-go" correspond, of course, to the "negative" and "expressive" meditations of the earlier discussion.

The not-doing or *wu-wei* pole is that defined by classical Yoga. In his *Yoga-aphorisms*, Patanjali says, "Yoga is the extinction of the movement of the mind." Not-doing may begin on the physical level with relaxation and then proceed to the subtler relaxation of attitude and thought. The medical, scientific theory of meditation in circulation today invokes only this *wu-wei* component of meditation. It comes from Herbert Benson, author of *The Relaxation Response*, who postulated that, just as there is an alarm response, there is also a regenerative response or mode of the organism akin to sleep (just as the stress response involves a sort of overwakefulness). I think we can explain meditation better in light of a multidimensional model in which the relaxation of body and mind constitute only one among several components.

Going even further, we may talk not only of components but of *dimensions* of meditation—just as in space we use dimensions to understand in a simple way the infinite multiplicity in the position of points. One of these dimensions is what I sometimes call the stop/go dimension, which involves the sphere of action; on one end of it I represent the calming of the mind (as in Yoga and Buddhist *samatha*), and on the other the attitude of allowing the free play of the mind, as I have discussed in *On the Psychology of Meditation* under the label of "Dionysian Way."

Furthermore, these two poles—that of calming the mind and that of letting it flow—are not opposites but a complementarity. Though logically opposite, they are experientially compatible—just as particle and wave may be grouped in physics as one beyond our physical models and mental maps. Thus good Zen not only involves inner silence but inner *freedom*, a permeability like that of the sky which, according to an old metaphor, permits the movement of birds and clouds.

Another dimension of meditation, in the theoretical perspective I am unfolding before you, spans a different polarity. One end of this I call "mindfulness": the practice of awareness to immediate experience. It may be the experience of the body or other sensory experience, of feeling experience, or of the thinking process. In all cases, we pay attention to the particulars of experience. It is typical of *vipassana*, for instance, and of other forms of meditation involving attention to the process of thinking.

At the other end or pole of this second division I place "God-mindedness," for here attention is focused not on the particulars of experience but on the mind itself; not on the "figure" but on the "ground" of experience. While in mindfulness attention is directed to sensations, feelings, "states of mind," in God-mindedness (which is the gist of what I called before "concentrative meditation") the focus is on symbolic material—whether a visual symbol such as a color or a flame, or a concept such as that of self, God, of divine attributes or qualities of enlightenment, or even the concept of emptiness. Something in these cases serves as a bridge between the mind and that which is beyond the particulars of experience, between the mind and its own depth. Just as in the former the task is one of focusing on detail, here the focus is on the experience of value, the experience of sacredness itself; it is not the *forms* of being that are the object, but being itself. This form of meditation can also be called *absorptive*, for the process begins with concentration and continues (spontaneously or intentionally) with an identification with the object, a *samadhi* in which the subject is not aware of itself as different from the mantram, the visualization, or the God-form evoked.

Just as not-doing and letting-go constitute a complementarity and not a contradiction, we may observe a complementarity between the two poles in this second, cognitive dimension: between attention to the world and the concrete, and attention to the root of consciousness; attention to the "figure" and the "ground" of experience. This is also a polarity between the *focusing* of attention and its widening in a "choiceless awareness" to the whole field of experience. This complementarity becomes manifest when we consider that mindfulness constitutes a possible approach to transcendence, and that those who have been touched by the experience of transcendence may experience an awakening to the world of ordinary perception as well.

We might think of these four processes or tasks that the meditator can embark upon as four internal gestures, four different ways of "putting oneself" inwardly. These four gestures of mind might be said also to constitute the *process* of meditation, for meditation consists in not-doing, in letting-go, in paying attention, and in evoking (or invoking) in different proportions. Some techniques have a predominantly calming effect; others partake more of the invocational quality, as worship; others may lie halfway between surrender and the concentrative effort. The domain of Kundalini Yoga, for instance, can be seen as a combination of mindfulness and God-mindedness: meditation on the chakras (body centers) involves mindfulness, for attention is focused on parts of the body that are not ordinarily in the foreground of awareness but in the background of experience (we are mostly aware of the surface of our bodies, and such meditation invites us to focus on the somewhat forgotten invisible center or axis of the body); yet together with this component of mindfulness there is also a deliberate invocation of divine attributes, different aspects of sacredness, that are superimposed on the chakras, as visualizations of the elements and colors, symbolic geometrical patterns, and with the support of mantra, gods and goddesses—all with the consequence of supporting the sense of the divine within.

Since the 1970 book I have published only a short paper on meditation (at the request of Dr. John R. Staude and the *Consciousness and Culture* magazine). In it (1970) I presented the same fourfold meditation map that I have shared with you thus far. Yet in this analysis I have not included in the realm of meditation the cultivation of love, and that omission introduces a rather questionable boundary between devotional practices and the rest of the meditation domain—particularly since I have included letting-go and God-mindedness, which are hardly separable from devotion in the life of prayer. For those who prefer to exclude devotional-ism from the sphere of meditation proper, what I will now pro-ceed to show will be more appropriately called a mapping of *spiritual exercises*, or an analysis of the dimensions of contempla-tive experience, rather than the dimensions of "meditation." Be this as it may be—a map of meditation or a map of spiritual exercises—I have in recent years chosen to include in my analysis the devotional path—Bakti Yoga in all its cultural and technical forms, including *guru bhakta* and practices for the development of compassion.

The view of this enlarged realm makes it clear (as I proposed for the first time at the meeting of the International Transper-sonal Association in Bombay in 1982) that meditation in a general sense of the word must be explained in reference to more than the not-doing/letting-go (conative) axis and the cognitive axis (along which are contrasted attention to the foreground and background of experience). We also need to introduce an emotional or *affective* axis in our map. I see this as spanning, like the other two, a complementarity of love and nonattachment. More exactly (since love is a word used for many things, including the all-too-human passions), "universal love" may be a more appropriate term for one end, while the other could also be evocatively de-scribed as "cosmic indifference." Just as it is obvious that love requires a background of nonattachment and is obscured by neediness as well as by hate, the converse is also true: it is love that, through its abundance, permits the relinquishing of clinging.

These six gestures of the mind, then, might be said to con-stitute the process of meditation. Thus far I have been speaking of the three dimensions of meditation as if they were completely independent of each other—just like the three dimensions of space, appropriately represented by the orthogonal coordinates of analytic geometry. This is only an approximation, however, for there is an affinity between the practices of not-doing, mindfulness, and nonattachment, and there is, likewise, a relationship between their opposite poles: letting-go, God-mindedness, and love. We may speak, in the case of the former three, of a "yogic complex"—for these are the attitudes most characteristic of Indian and Buddhist Yoga (and, generally speaking, of Far Eastern spirituality); in the other three we may recognize the "religious complex"—that is, the constellation of practices characteristic of religion in the Western sense of the term and shared by Judaism, Christianity, Islam, and Indian devotionalism.

These two predominant orientations in spiritual practice, sometimes called the "dry" and the "wet" ways, or the "solar" and "lunar" paths, are not incompatible, however, as is historically demonstrated by the combination of both in Sufism and Tantrism and the considerable elaboration of both in Tibetan Buddhism.

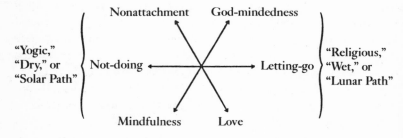

Figure 1

If these are six processes or components of the meditation process, we can go even deeper and say that these are six different aspects of one single underlying process.

Now that we have represented the basic psychological exercises as the vertices of the hexagram in Figure 1, we may represent this additional idea by drawing from these corners lines that converge at the tip of a pyramid. This tip will stand for a common process of suspension of what is in the mind like a veil ob-

structing spiritual experience. Usually in spiritual discourse this
is called the "ego."*

We could say that not-doing, to the extent that it brings everything to a stop in the psyche, is a natural remedy for anything
that may be going wrong; whatever the dynamics, whatever our
habits, emotions, and thoughts, if we only manage to stop whatever we are doing that is dysfunctional, we are momentarily
healthy. So the calming of the mind—*samatha* in Buddhist
terminology—is like a grinding against the ego. Calming the
mind helps us regardless of the kind of compulsive behavior that
permeates our psyche.

Yet, since the ego is a great obstructor, letting-go can also be
ego-poison. One of the facets of the ego may be described as a
usurpation of a control belonging to the whole of the mind by
what may be viewed as an island in the psyche.

In connection with the letting-go of control, I want to bring in
the concept of organismic self-regulation. This biological concept, which became widespread through Fritz Perls and Gestalt
therapy, constitutes a modern echo of the old idea of Tao. Just as
in Tao and Tê there is the notion that by yielding to an inner spontaneity the individual acts in harmony with the world, I believe
that organismic self-regulation, when allowed to operate, leads to
precisely this harmony. We say that we are designed in such a
way that, if we function properly, we find ourselves in harmony
with something beyond us—whereas, if this regulation of the
whole by the whole is inhibited (and it is the "little man" inside
who is in control), then we lack the fluidity and complexity that
are within our potential, the "little mind" that has to make deci-
sions through the operation of conceptual thinking alone.

*This ego of Hinduism, Buddhism, and Transpersonal Psychology is not that of
contemporary psychoanalysis but corresponds to the psychological notion of
"character," as the sum of conditionings—the mechanical part of our nature with
which we ordinarily identify: learned ways of doing, seeing, and perceiving,
endowed with a false sense of self and which stand in the way of a more fluid and
creative alternative to life within our potential.

Another aspect of the ego is unconsciousness—an *active* unconsciousness. If a part regulates the whole, it must do so at the expense of repression; it must block awareness and block impulse. To keep something from expression, it has to ignore it. That was the Freudian discovery; and the Freudian discovery of the unconscious is parallel to the Buddhist insight to the extent that there is *avidya*, an active unconsciousness, or "ignorance" operating in the mind. Through this unconsciousness the personality is fragmented and comes to see itself as separated from the whole. It is as if the links between mental events are not there and the contents of experience are not properly organized. And so we can say that mindfulness—awareness—is an antidote for this active unconsciousness; in restoring awareness and cultivating contact with immediate experience, the psychological inertia of the ego is counteracted.

Something similar can be said about God-mindedness, which is also an antidote to the ego because in the functioning of the ego there is not only a closing down, a veiling over of perception, a fragmentation, but especially a loss of *meaning*, a loss of value. Dante expressed this in the *Divine Comedy* by making hell—the realm of emotional sickness—inaccessible to angels. (Angels move about in heaven and purgatory but, with a single exception, they don't come into hell.) I think this is a good metaphor for the fact that the mechanical mind of the ego, which is like a puppet, a computer, or a life-simulation, doesn't have a place for the mystery of existence.

The ego might be called a false-self. It is something that calls itself "self" and, precisely because it is not the fullness of our being, it contains, more or less veiled, the experience of a lack of being and also a *thirst* for being. The ego has *apparent* being, is an apparent personality, but to the extent we are of the ego, we are really trying to be, *wanting* to be. We would like to be more alive, we would like to be full, and it is this thirst for being that moves us to do most of what we do. From this thirst for being and the corresponding threat of nonbeing comes the craving, the anger, the need always to keep things out. We might say that the blood that runs in the veins of ego is this craving, this thirst; while the "blood of being"—of the soul, the true self, the essence—is abundance, which is to say love. And if we consider that love, the sense of abundance and overflowing, is a part of both health and of enlightenment, we may understand the activation of love as a movement away from the limitations of a deficiency-motivated ego.

And the same may be said of nonattachment: it is, like the other ingredients of meditative disciplines, a method for the suspension of the ego—for the ego, rooted in craving, cannot practice nonattachment (except through self-inhibition).

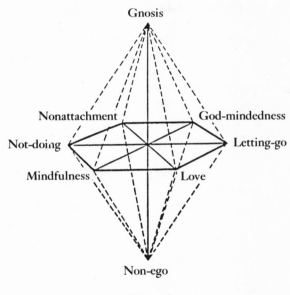

Figure 2*

*The appropriate geometrical representation of nonindependent dimensions is that of nonorthogonal coordinates—the angles between them a measure of their intercorrelation—and I have sought to express this through the elongation of the hexagonal base of the double pyramid in Figure 2, itself a two-dimensional representation of the three partially independent axes.

It only remains for me to explain why I have now changed the pyramid thus far described to a double pyramid: to convey that the six gestures of the mind that converge on the suspension of the ego also meet as so many facets of the deep meditative consciousness that constitutes the other side of egolessness. Thus far we have only dwelt on the negative side of meditative experience. It is time we pay attention to the other side as well and say that the goal of meditation is not only the suspension of the ego but also spiritual experience. In Buddhism we have both words: *nirvana*, pointing to extinction (the suspension of "samsaric" consciousness and the passions) and also *sambodhi*, "enlightenment" or awakening. Also in the Sufi tradition we find the corresponding pair, *fana* (annihilation) and *baqa* (permanence).

Thus in Figure 2 I have written "non-ego" at the bottom of the vertical axis and "gnosis" at the top, to indicate spiritual perception, the perception of what is behind the veil of ego, the knowing of Reality by Itself in which the individual may partake when the clouds of obscuration are dispersed.

6 / The Interface Between
Meditation and Psychotherapy

The coming together of the spiritual and the therapeutic is a subject that reflects a most important aspect of the spirit of our time. It is a subject that also reflects my own career, since from the time of my coming to the United States from Chile in the 1960s my occupation has been something halfway between these two fields; I have advocated bringing meditation into the therapeutic endeavor.

My subject will be the communality between both domains rather than their differences. I think that some of the differences have to do with our use of words. For instance, when it is said that meditation "dissolves the ego" and would be dangerous for persons who have not formed an ego, I think there is a confusion between the ego of psychoanalysis and the ego of the spiritual traditions. The ego that the spiritual traditions undertake to dissolve is not that entity which is a mediating and adaptive instance in the psyche. I think that this *ahamkara*, in identifying with which we forget our identity with universal being, is more closely related to what we today call character: the system of

Adapted from opening talk at the Conference for Meditation and Psychotherapy, 1988.

obsolete programs that we build in our early life. It is a not uncommon idea in psychotherapy today that we should transcend character. For instance, Fritz Perls used to say that the ideal person is a person without character. Character is an "armor" or straitjacket acquired in early life, not *rigor mortis* but *rigor vitae*, and today the transpersonal movement has taken up this idea of a creative response to life rather than remaining bound by early conditioning.

Also, when we talk about the goals of therapy and the goals of meditation, I think that the formulated goals are not as important as what is actually *done*. I think most of therapy has been exercised under the umbrella of theories that have less to do with its practice than is assumed. Therapy purports to be the implementation of a theory, but actually that is mostly not the case: the theory comes later. We have yet to discover the real theory of psychotherapy; perhaps it is very similar to the theory of meditation.

Today we are discovering not only the therapeutic relevance of meditation but the spiritual relevance of psychotherapy, and I think that the process of growth is actually a holistic one in which the psychological and the spiritual are like two ends of a single stick. When we discover the therapeutic relevance of the spiritual traditions, we are not really discovering something new but *re*discovering something that was implicit in their origins. For instance, I had a teacher, Chu Fang Chu, who was a Taoist, a student of the seventy-second patriarch in Taoism. He had come to California with the exodus of so many other Chinese, and I invited him to work with my group. I had many students in the early 1970s who were highly interested in spiritual things. Chu Fang Chu wanted to emphasize to our group that "we Taoists are not so concerned with spiritual things like you people; for us the most important thing is health. We are concerned with the healing of the energy process in the body. When the circulating of the energy in the smaller orbit and the greater orbit is healed, the subtler aspects of the individual are also healed."

Buddhism, too, if we regard it in the words of the Buddha, could be called therapeutic, because the emphasis of the Buddha was on helping people with suffering. He was an expert in making people aware of suffering and a pioneer in the understanding that realizing the universality and pervasiveness of suffering is part of the cure. So really one of the most important aspects of Buddhism is that of developing equanimity (*upekkn*) in the middle of suffering.

I will elaborate on the idea that healing and enlightenment are two aspects of a single thing. We may be tempted to think that healing is the more humble facet, the first level, and that enlightenment is the later level; but I think that even that is only an approximation. When we hear that Jesus conquered the devil just at the last moment before beginning to teach, or that Buddha vanquished the temptation of Mara on the day of Enlightenment under the bodhi tree, we are being told that the ego persists until the very last stage of illumination (I do not think the devil is very different from the principle of *samsara* or *spirite obsanmit* at the heart of all psychopathology).

I will deal with the subject of the contact or interfaces of meditation and therapy in connection with different facets of meditation, because I see meditation as a many-faceted phenomenon. I have even developed what could be called a many-dimensional theory of meditation, a theory according to which meditation is the intersection of different dimensions of the psyche [see the preceding essay, "For a Theory of Meditation: An Update"]. Instead of restating this theory contemplating the psychological relevance of meditation here, however, I will share with you the essentials of it as we go along, and the outlines of the theory will become obvious after I deal with the different subjects.

To begin, let me postulate that there is in meditation a dimension that has to do with the polarity of stopping the mind and letting the mind go. In *On the Psychology of Meditation* (1970) I spoke of the "Apollonian" and "Dionysian" aspects. Some types of meditation emphasize concentration of the mind on one spot.

Other types emphasize surrender. In the beginning of the aphorisms of Patanjali (which have to do with the Apollonian way), we are told of "the stopping of the vibrations of the mind" or "extinction of the movement of the mind," *citavritti nirodha*, but Patanjali says at the very beginning that there is another way, which is *Ishvara pranidhana*, "surrender to the Lord." On the whole when people speak of meditation there is an implicit connotation of the stopping of the mind.

On the Psychology of Meditation was criticized on the grounds that this "letting-go" had little to do with meditation, but I think I am speaking here to an audience that is very aware of "dynamic meditation," which emphasizes something that is present (in an implicit way) even in the old yogic forms of meditation. Buddhism, for instance, typically emphasizes the development of stillness and of a sharp awareness, but the complete practice of Buddhism comprises taking refuge in which the practitioner surrenders to the Buddha, the *Dharma*, and the *Sangha*. Buddha, *Dharma*, and *Sangha* are interpreted on several levels. For instance, surrender to the *Dharma* means surrender not only to the teachings but to the sustaining principle of the universe—thus, relinquishing control and accepting that the universe runs itself. (the word *Dharma* derives from *dhr*, "sustenance, support"). It is not different from the ideas of Tao, the will of God, and the idea is present in every form of spirituality, although in the Christian tradition and in Islam it is a matter of surrendering to God; in Taoism, to a deeper spontaneity.

So even in Zen, in which apparently the interest is in quietude, stillness, and concentration, the true understanding of the ultimate state is one in which there is a complementarity of calm and permeability or inner freedom. As in the metaphor of the sixth patriarch, this means letting the mind be as space, which doesn't interfere with any of the bodies in it, or letting the mind be as the sky, in which the clouds can move.

If we think of psychotherapy in terms of this polarity, it is obvious that all of it has much to do with letting-go. The story of psychotherapy begins with Anton Mesmer, because Freud was inspired by hypnosis. Mesmer's discovery was that in hypnotic trance people can surrender more and a self-healing comes into operation, a self-regenerative force. Freud in his early work tried to mimic hypnosis, and his free association was a way of inviting the spontaneous course of thought liberated from social constraints. If we look at Freud's description of free association in his later years, we see that it is very similar to meditation, because it consists in not only awareness but the free flow of thought, an attitude of not interfering with thought.

But if we go further into the story of psychotherapy, we see more and more emphasis on the liberation of impulses. Freud did not believe in the loss of restraint but believed in an ultimate incompatibility between instinct and civilization only in the undoing of repression, in the sense of allowing the content of the unconscious into consciousness. It was Wilhelm Reich who believed in the liberation of instinct. To the liberation characteristic of the new therapies in the humanistic movement, Fritz Perls (and others) contributed a much greater daring in the sense of undoing not only the repressed but the suppressed—that is, liberating not only awareness but impulse. In Gestalt therapy this undoing of inhibitions is not an aim in itself, however, but a means to becoming aware of impulses in the act of expression. Also, J. L. Moreno emphasized psychotherapy as an education in spontaneity.

We could cite many more examples, but I think it is obvious that if we are to theorize about psychotherapy, the principle of letting-go is one of its pillars. What is not so clear is the complementary aspect that is so emphasized in meditation: that of stopping—stopping the mind, or "stopping the world" if we want to use Carlos Castaneda's language. It is present in therapy most explicitly in the form of relaxation (the popular cure for stress)—physical relaxation and the relaxation of the mind that is supported by physical relaxation. The stopping of conceptualization has also come into psychotherapy, mostly with Gestalt.

I think this idea of stopping the ego, stopping the agitation of the passions, is a fertile idea to bring into psychotherapy. The more an individual matures, the more there is a spontaneous learning of *wu-wei*, a way of being that is less deliberate, in which' he is not telling himself what to do and what not to do. A perfect individual is somebody who in some sense *is lived by his life*. (We cannot separate spontaneity and inspiration from the stopping of what in the psyche constitutes its obstacle.) I think therapy is more aware of the Dionysian aspect of this polarity, while spiritual practitioners are more aware of the contribution of inner silence to mental development.

In view of still another dimension of meditation, we find a polarity so that some types of meditation emphasize one or the other end of it. In this case too we may say that a complementarity is at play, and that in both cases we find processes that reflect an ultimate state that transcends them. One pole of this complementarity we can call mindfulness, perhaps best represented by *vipassana* and by Middle Eastern practices of attention to daily life. This too is very familiar to psychotherapy, particularly in the humanistic movement; because, even though psychoanalysis began with an emphasis on the past, it led to increasing emphasis on the ongoing transference situation. Also, as it moved from past to present it moved from intellectual understanding to immediate awareness, and in Gestalt therapy (which became the source of the universalization of the here-and-now in humanistic psychology) the emphasis is not only on the significance of being aware of this or that, but on the restoration of awareness itself. This awareness is our birthright, we may say; it is an aspect of a healthy consciousness that needs to be restored. The emphasis on awareness can be found in many therapies, ranging from the practice of encounter (in which people are educated in being sensitive to their ongoing feelings toward each other) to many of the body therapies—which might be called forms of spiritual work through the body.

Just as there is a kind of spiritual practice in which we are invited to know that we are moving our left foot or that we are breathing in, and how, there is another form of meditation and spiritual practice in which we are invited to bring awareness away from the world of perceptions, emotions, and thoughts, away from the differentiated foreground of mental processes, toward the center of the mind itself, toward the very source of awareness. While this may be done directly, it is most commonly done through the mediation of symbols—such as the conceptual symbol "god." Even in Buddhism, where the doctrine speaks of the ultimate nonexistence of self, there is a practice of looking at "who is looking" and an invitation to understand the essence of the mind beyond mental phenomena.

Just as visual mandala-like symbols may invite the mind toward its center, the same may be said of sound. The traditional Indian expression *shabda brahman* ("sound is God") expresses and invites the experience, and mantra gives it articulation. Mantra involves phonetic symbolism. Just as the color red conveys a different atmosphere from the color blue, so different phonetic qualities symbolize different aspects of the divine (or, if you prefer, aspects of enlightened consciousness). Training in this kind of meditation begins with concentration—exercises in one-pointedness—and proceeds to the visualization of divinities with manifold characteristics and spiritual attributes. Finally, it comprises practices that culminate in the "incorporation" of the mind-created divinities into the practitioner's body and mind. This method exists not only in the Tantric traditions but in the Christian, in which the sacrament of communion may be seen as a reinstatement of the Egyptian sacrament of self-divinization through god-eating.

All this can be called *absorptive meditation*. We may speak of an absorption of the meditation-object into the subject, or absorbing oneself in the contemplation of the object. In either case there is a *samadhi* in which there is no subject-object differentiation.

It is easy to see the method of exercising awareness of mindfulness in psychotherapy; it is not so easy to see this complementarity of absorption—which is fully expressed in visionary trance. It is present, however—in the Jungian approach, for instance—and in work with creative visualization (often inspired by it). I have said many times that Jung's main contribution to psychology is to have smuggled in the traditional gods under the acceptable label of archetypes. The traditional idea is that there is a healing effect of spiritual experience, a "healing through the spirit." There is abundant testimony as to how seeing God can have seemingly miraculous healing repercussions. All our spiritual and psychological thirst is quenched when we have this great satisfaction of spiritual experience. An important object of the Jungian approach is that of inviting the contemplation of archetypes (and "archetypes" are not different from "religious symbols"). Jung's invitation to contemplate our ordinary life from an archetypal perspective—i.e., as an intersection of great forces beyond the human world—should have the same effect, I think, as the recommendation in the Jewish tradition, "If you want to come to God, fill your head with God"—we may say, "be God-minded."

Because the principle of awareness is obvious in psychotherapy but the idea of orientation toward "a beyond" is something that seems to have been left behind as a Christian anachronism in the secularized West, I think it makes sense to emphasize the therapeutic implications of traditional religious practices. Yet "God-centeredness" need not be bound to Christian religiosity or even to a theistic outlook, for there are those who are not, intellectually speaking, believers and yet have a potential for mystical experience. In such cases I think the best vehicle to develop the sense of holiness is music. Of course, there are ways and ways of listening to music, and how we listen may be even more important than what we listen to. That is why beyond the acknowledged realm of musical therapy (the very existence of which speaks for the recognition of the healing properties of music and in which practically no emphasis is given to the "art of listening") there lies a wide realm of "music as meditation"—a use of music in which only its evocative content is taken into account and which emphasizes what we can do with it.

Among the many ways in which music can be taken as a meditation object, of special relevance with regard to our subject of god-mindedness is what I usually speak of as the use of music listening as *dhikr*. The word *dhikr* in Sufism translates both as "repetition" and as "remembrance," and both words are appropriate with reference to the traditional technique that consists in the sustained remembrance of God through the repetition of a verbal formula (such as *la illaha illa l allah*). It was the original function of music to express and induce spiritual experience, precisely through its lending an implicit support for concentration on the divine. There are sophisticated ways in which we may do this, sometimes employing music to invoke specific attributes of the divine, but it is enough to suggest to the psychotherapy patient to explore "music listening as worship."

I have talked about a conative dimension of meditation that has to do with letting-go or stopping. Then I talked about a cognitive aspect, which orients itself either to the cultivation of a panoramic attention directed to the world of mental events or a focused attention aimed at the center of the mind. Yet, if we talk about meditation in a broad sense we also need to consider an *affective* dimension, and here we find a polarity of love and nonattachment. This is a seeming contradiction but really a complementarity, for you cannot have true love without the transcendence of attachment, and on the other hand, a selfless attitude is stimulated by the gift of love. Since the two are mutually supportive, it is understandable that both simultaneously are recommended in Mahayana Buddhism, with its ideal of nonattachment and compassion.

Psychotherapy, of course, is intimately concerned with love in that the attempt to restore health cannot be conceived as different from that of restoring the ability to love—itself inseparable from healthy relationships and happiness. That this is a goal of psychotherapy may need to be emphasized today, when in the hu-

manistic psychology movement so much practical emphasis has
been given to the catharsis and sharing of anger. Important as
this is, it is sometimes taken to be an end in itself rather than
understood as a necessary step toward the acknowledgment of
"one's shadow"—and, eventually, the healing of childish ambiv-
alence.

Particularly relevant to the restoration of the human capacity
to love is, I think, the therapy originated by Robert Hoffman
(Fisher-Hoffman or Quadrinity therapy), which undertakes to
restore the individual's ability to love himself and others through
a process comprising first the catharsis of primitive anger toward
one's parents and then the process of forgiving them. Whatever
the means by which the ability to relate nondestructively is pursued in psychotherapy, however, I think that the formula of com-
plementing the endeavor with the practice of nonattachment
through meditation is particularly desirable.

To speak of love, however, implies more than the love toward
fellow beings. It comprises not only the love of beauty and the
love of ideas but, at the highest end of the love continuum, the
love toward the supreme or love of sacredness as is expressed in
the activity of worship. When Jesus asserted that all the commandments could be summarized as one, that of loving God
above all things and one's neighbor as one's self, he truly was not
stating one prescription for life but implicitly three: that of loving God above all else, that of loving one's self, and that of loving
others no less. In this threefold formula for the practice of love,
only the human aspects are taken into account by psychotherapy,
while typically the spiritual traditions have emphasized loving
God and the active love of seeking the absolute. We may say that
it is easier to love God than to love a human being in that the love
of the ideal does not lead to the frustration of loving the imperfect: we may say that to love God is human while to love humans
is divine. Perhaps the great religious teachers of the past implicitly knew that love for the ultimate is a fountain for the love
of people in general, in that it is a universal occasion to awaken
one's own capacity for loving Being beyond individual beings.

Such considerations, too, incline us to consider the usefulness of a transpersonal context to psychotherapy along with the usefulness of a practice in nonattachment. I have already spoken of the relevance of God-centeredness, "God-mindedness," and here add a remark about the practical inseparability between the purely cognitive aspect of God-mindedness and the affective aspect of devotion as expressed through such traditional forms as Bakhti Yoga and prayer in the Judeo-Christian tradition. Also *guru bakhta*, the traditional cultivation of devotion toward a spiritual teacher (embodied in St. Paul's assertion that one can only come to know the Father through the Son) is something which I think psychotherapy has disparaged one-sidedly as a collusion between immaturity and narcissistic exploitativeness, and yet it may be reconsidered as a valid cultivation of love toward an ideal object, at least in a situation where the spiritual guide is truly closer to the spiritual world than the one guided.

Thus far we have been able to perceive a relevance of each one of the components of meditation of psychotherapy: relaxation in both its aspect of noninterference and in that of allowing for effortless calm; attention both to ever-changing mental events and to the ever-present though dark background of consciousness; love of persons and love of the transpersonal. It only remains to explore now the interface between psychotherapy and nonattachment. I think this is of special interest today in that psychotherapy has become so concerned with the problem of self-inhibition and socially conditioned self-interference that the aspect of self-control implied by austerity has caused psychotherapy to be implicitly suspicious of the asceticism characteristic of traditional spirituality.

Yet asceticism is as old as shamanism and exists in the context of an explicit or implicit ideal of becoming (as the Bhagavad Gita puts it) "the same in pleasure and in pain." Asceticism is almost a synonym for spiritual practice in traditional Western religion and exists everywhere in spirituality from ancient Hatha Yoga to modern Islam. It is usually associated (whether in the Upanishads or in the perception of the Pythagoreans) with the ideal of a separation between soul and body. Since contemporary thinking is more interested in the ultimate unity between the physical and the psychological, and little credence is given in it to the idea of a separate soul, this shift in thinking has contributed to the prevalent view today of asceticism and austerity as a thing of the past—possibly a masochistic phenomenon—or merely a way of propitiating an imaginary parent in heaven.

I think we should draw a distinction, which traditional religions fail to draw, between the passions and the body, the passions being the realm of the ego, and the body the vehicle of healthy animal instinct. The human predicament, and particularly the neurotic predicament, is that of being a prisoner of passions such as greed, pride, and envy while at the same time being instinctually unfree. Both instinctual freedom and liberation from such forms of deficiency motivation as the passions occur in the process of successful insight psychotherapy.

Yet I think that in this matter again we need not consider the practice and ideal of nonattachment as incompatible with the therapeutic injunction to *become* one's emotions, express them and heed them in the therapeutic process. It is the "unnatural" or pathological passions and not the natural drives that are the objective enemy of the spiritually unfolding individual, and I think that not only insight but the active practice of inhibiting their expression is appropriate to transcending them. This is what is traditionally done through the practice of "virtue"—commandments or injunctions spelling out virtue being ultimately forms of what we may call ego continuance. Yet the inhibition of neurotic needs may take more creative forms in contemporary psychotherapy. While engaging in active efforts is a part of behavior modification today, I think it may be fruitful to consider that every effort to bypass one's conditioned behavior patterns involves, at a subtle but fundamental level, the practice of nonattachment in the face of the underlying impulses.

In addition to what may be said concerning the development of ego strength and the capacity of forbearance in daily life, I think that nonattachment can also be the object of specific personal psychological exercises and psychotherapeutic applications.

Throughout my teaching experience, I have implemented a belief that both mindfulness and God-mindedness need to be cultivated (as they are in the *vajrayana* and in Sufism). The pursuit of mindfulness through practices such as *vipassana* and Gestalt therapy need not exclude God-mindfulness, be it in the form of a transpersonal context, special techniques of meditation with an object, and the learning of creative journeying in trance. Both are poorly developed or pathologically obscured, so neither do we know the depth of our minds nor are we fully awake to our perception of the world and our bodies. We need to be more in touch with heaven and with earth at the same time—to cultivate our connection with the Cosmic Parent and also the domain of consciousness that we call self.

7 / Music as Meditation and Therapy

Music can be meditation for the composer, for the performer, and for the listener: yet because not everybody is a performer and few are composers while everybody is a listener, it is music listening that I will now take on as my subject. Not only can music audition become meditation through a deliberate attempt and through the use of a particular technique; we may say that the best of musical listening is already meditation, in that it involves a putting aside of one's "worldly self" (and a projection onto the music of a measure of implicit spiritual content) and also a measure of identification with it.

Perhaps music would not be as important as it has been shown to be throughout the history of humankind if it did not constitute a sort of spiritual nourishment and an occasion for a state of mind that we regard as highly valuable. There are those for whom music is already a spiritual vehicle and a healing influence, and they do not need further techniques. In what follows, however, I will share ways in which we may deliberately experiment with musical listening so as to actualize its spiritual possibilities, and suggest "spiritual audition" experiences.

In speaking of "music as meditation," I do not necessarily imply that we are to use music as a substitute for silent meditation;

for audition, unlike visualization or active ritual, might be regarded as an extrinsically stimulated meditation. Because of this,
music has been considered by some spiritual teachers as something not to be abused or given priority. Perhaps comparable to
psychedelics in its mysticomimetic or ecstatogenic potential, music, I think, should be regarded as the "salt and pepper" of meditation rather than its "bread and butter": a special stimulus, a
special psychospiritual lubricant on which we should not become
dependent. Ideally, music should be a counterpoint to the pursuit
through silent meditation of that self-supportive and yet
nowhere-supported condition most characteristic of meditative
depth.

There are nonspecific ways in which we may use music as a
stimulus for meditation. We may find it to be a useful background
for relaxation, for instance. The soothing content of music in
this situation is enhanced by the perception of a sort of sound
cocoon around the listener—a sound-filled sector in space that is
most conducive to self-abandon into a "fetuslike" regression,
a deep relaxation of the action and spring orientation of the
ordinary mind.

Perhaps a more specific music-related kind of meditation,
however, is that which rests on the equation of sound with the
divine (in the widest sense of the word). However true it may be
that light is the most frequent symbol of the divine in the codified
language of the religions, we may say that hearing is of greater
mystical import than seeing; and sound (and its modulation) is a
more potent vehicle for the sense of the holy that anything in the
visual world.

Because in listening to music we may be tempted to expect that
music "does it for us"—that is to say, we may be inclined to
passively (psychoanalytically speaking, "orally") expect to be
filled, satisfied, and pleased by music to the point of ecstasy—and
because all of this is contrary to the attitude most conducive to
the deep musical contemplation, I think it is most appropriate to
begin the exploration of music as a devotional vehicle through

sound itself. For if sound be Brahman, as the old saying *shabda brahman* asserts, this is not something to which we are ordinarily attuned. The Chandogya Upanishad tells us that Brahman is to be found in the sound of fire that may be heard by closing one's ears. I propose this exercise as a beginning of its exploration: meditation on the divine by means of sharply and subtly listening to the sound in the depth of one's ears. Those who carry out this exercise will probably be interested in exploring another Indian practice that involves not only listening but utterance: the evocation of sacredness through the chanting of the syllable *om*. The most appropriate way of doing so is by singing it in the lowest possible register (evocative of the widest space), and in such a way as to generate as many harmonics as possible (evocative of experiential density).

When we apply the principle of evocation through sound to the listening of music proper, I think that the best practice to be recommended for a Westerner may be that of listening to Indian classical music, which unfolds in the ever-sustained presence of its tonic (usually played by the tamboura)—a musical correlate of the presence of the divine.

Aside from the suitability of Indian music for concentration on the divine by virtue of its structure, where melody and rhythm are supported by a drone, it is appropriate for another reason. For some people at least, too strong an associative relationship has been established between the Western musical repertoire and states of mind that lie within the bounds of the ordinary if not the morbid. If it is true that lack of familiarity with the different music language of Indian classical music can be a limitation at the beginning, I think that the educational experience of continuing familiarization is worth its rewards; for, as in the use of ecclesiastical Latin and Sanskrit, Indian music can afford a purely "liturgical" medium—i.e., one dedicated by us to evoke specifically extramundane experience.

Moving a step further in the direction of tapping the more specific potential of music, we can now turn our attention from listening to the divine "in general" to listening to particular divine attributes: particular nuances of spiritual experience that are reflected in specific compositions. This aspect of music is well known in the Indian culture, where each traditional *raga* (a sound sequence that constitutes the melodic seed-structure of a composition) has relation to a particular angle of the sun above the horizon and a specific internal state and is considered appropriate to play only within certain hours. Obviously, since music is evocative of internal states, we may employ it as a stimulus for more deliberately eliciting these states, just as in the case of mantra.

Yet our own musical heritage is rich in expressions of the highest consciousness—much beyond, I think, what Western seekers have become aware of or acknowledged. What Bach represents in the world's musical history cannot be separated from what he represents in the history of the expression of holiness, no matter what limitations the composer may have shared with his time and society. (From such limitations not even the saints are exempt.) Thus, we may want to try Bach's *"Erbarme dich"* aria in the *Passion According to St. Matthew* as a stimulus to the contemplation of Divine Compassion. Or we may seek to become absorbed in the joyousness of the "Divine Child" through the Allegro of Mozart's Sonata K. 238 in G.

Before saying anything further about the use of Western music as a means of concentration on the divine, however, I want to address myself to how appropriate it is to consider the best of what is ostensibly "secular" music (of recent centuries in the West) as religious. I believe that although *musica sacra* and *musica profana* went their different ways (so that post-baroque was first addressed to the court and later to the bourgeoisie and to all people and yet kept outside the church), it is secular music that has truly realized to the farthest the potential of music for expressing and inspiring the divine.

The discrepancy between acknowledged and real spiritual relevance has been, I think, the effect of one-sidedness in the patriarchal Western world. Classicism and romanticism, which followed the baroque, were not a step backward but forward in the unfolding of consciousness—away from father dominance in the psyche and in society, forward toward the feminine principle, related to embodiment and to the earth rather than to the "heavenly." We may say, in agreement with Hermann Sherchen (in *The Nature of Music*) that Beethoven was "the inventor of European music," for he used it as language for the expression of a different realm of experience than earlier music. Music may have always expressed "experience," yet in Bach we may say that this is the intuition of the "music of the heavenly spheres," the "music of the macrocosm," as Totila Albert used to call it, in contraposition to the "music of the microcosm," truly human music that Beethoven introduced and the romantics continued to compose.

And then there is Brahms.

Hans von Bülow used to say humorously that, of the "three Bs" of music, Bach was the Father, Beethoven the Son, and Brahms the Holy Spirit. I think that his statement contained much truth, in that we find in Bach the highest expression of the sense of God as father in Western music, while Beethoven expresses the voice of the individual human or son throughout his quest, and Brahms has given us a supreme musical expression of the "universal mother" and of mother love.

I think that we have tended to regard music as "mere music" and its composers as "mere musicians," when the fact is that music is potentially a bridge between a heart that found itself and the heart of the listener.

Notwithstanding the fact that Bach has been frequently looked upon as an enlightened being and one of the "just," the case is very different with Beethoven, the rebel who wouldn't bow to the great of this earth or even to heaven itself (he expired pointing his fist upward to the thunder that then reached his ear). Because his music has generally been heard as "pure music"—that is to say, a music resting in an abstract aesthetic perfection, and perhaps rarely as the voice of one near to God—it may be useful to read what Elizabeth Brentano quotes Beethoven as saying:

When I open my eyes I must sigh, for what I see is contrary to my religion, and I must despise the world which does not know that music is a higher revelation than all wisdom and philosophy, the wine which inspires one to new generative processes, and I am the Bacchus who presses out this glorious wine for mankind and makes them spiritually drunken. When they are again become sober they have drawn from the sea all that they brought with them, all that they can bring with them to dry land. I have not a single friend, I must live alone. But well I know that God is nearer to me than to other artists; I associate with Him without fear; I have always recognized and understood Him and have no fear for my music—it can meet no evil fate. Those who understand it must be freed by it from all the miseries which the others drag about with themselves.

Music, verily, is the mediator between intellectual and sensuous life.

Speak to Goethe about me. Tell him to hear my symphonies and he will say that I am right in saying that music is the one incorporeal entrance into the higher world of knowledge which comprehends mankind but which mankind cannot comprehend.

It is well known among musicians and music scholars that Beethoven's work can be divided into three distinct periods: In the first it resembles that of Mozart and Haydn. In the second it has been interpreted by N. W. N. Sullivan and others as the expression of a struggle with himself. In the third (from the Ninth Symphony onward) he is most original and conveys the beatific bliss and brotherly love of one who obtained liberation. Those who want to absorb something of Beethoven's consciousness in this last period may explore, for instance, the "Song of gratitude to God by one healing" from his penultimate quartet, Op. 132.

My appreciation of Brahms as a star in the musical heavens of no lesser magnitude than Beethoven and Bach developed from both my experience in piano playing and from the influence of Totila Albert, who regarded Brahms as an invisible saint gifted with the destiny of a spontaneous psychological balance comparable to that which Beethoven achieved after long labors. Totila

Albert was one who, like Beethoven, experienced "self-birth" after many years of struggle, and as homage to Beethoven he conceived the re-creation of Beethoven's spiritual experience in
words. This led to a tapping into of what he used to call a music
dictation that was not his interpretation but the reflection of an
objective content conveyed by the music's structure. This dictation, which began with Beethoven, led him to a similar "de-
coding" of those in Beethoven's lineage, culminating in Brahms,
and it was Brahms to whom he devoted most of his work from
there on, for in him he saw the most evolved expression of the
balance between "father," "mother," and "child" within the human psyche. While Western music itself was to him the supreme
expression of drama in European culture and "the voice of
Three"—i.e., the voice of our threefold essence or soul—in
Brahms, Totila Albert saw an expression of an equilibrium representing an evolutionary leap away from a patriarchal imbalance.
Just as Beethoven reflected the French and other revolutions, we
sense that again there is a revolution of consciousness manifest in
the transition from Beethoven to Brahms.

Just as the king-centered world of Bach reflects an imprint of
the submissive psyche of authoritarian Christianity, and just as
Beethoven's music reflects a rebellion against established au-
thority, in Brahms, it seems to us, we hear a perfect synthesis of
his two great predecessors as well as a synthesis between the
classical and the romantic spirit. He is, as it were, the fruit of the
tree of which Bach is the trunk, a fruit (amidst the foliage of
romanticism) that was to fall and decompose as we moved into a
time of creation of new musical languages.

Not only is Bach present as a hidden spinal cord in Brahms's
music, but so is the spiral pattern of Beethoven's musical thinking
and, at the experiential level, the emphasis on individual experience characteristic of music from Beethoven onward. Brahms's
music, like that of Beethoven, contains the heartbeat, the acceler-
ations of the breath, that convey individual embodiment. Is this
not the expression of an imminently synthesizing gift and quality

of the mind, a gift of all-embracing reconciliation? At least it is obvious that his is the ripest and healthiest expression of love in classical music—a love that is both selfless and emblematic (I might say in concordance with Totila Albert) of a harmonious interweaving of father-mother-and-child love.

Thinking in this manner, I naturally want to include, in this statement on music as a vehicle for psychospiritual unfoldment, a recommendation of exploring Brahms further. I would recommend, for instance, listening to the first movement of his early Sextet Op. 18 as a "flying carpet" for a meditation on love—a love at the same time erotic, cosmic, and fraternal.

Or I would suggest becoming the two who dialogue (through the music of orchestra and piano respectively) in the second movement of his First Piano Concerto, Op. 15.

More importantly, however, if you are interested in exploring Brahms as a vehicle for consciousness extension, I suggest that you seek a connection with the mind of the creator behind his creations. Seek the presence of Brahms's mind beyond his notes, and make Brahms your guide—opening your ears to what, without words, he is saying.

Notes

INTRODUCTION

1. For my discussion of this point, see *The One Quest* (to be published).
2. I have done this to some extent in the article "Contributions of Gestalt Therapy," in *Ways of Growth* (New York: The Viking Press, 1969).

CHAPTER 1.

1. Richard of St. Victor, *De Gratia Contemplationis seu Benjamin Major*, I, 3, in *Selected Writings on Contemplation*, tr. Claire Kirchberger (London: 1957).
2. Philip Kapleau, ed., *The Three Pillars of Zen: Teaching, Practice and Enlightenment* (Boston: Beacon Press, 1965).

CHAPTER 2.

1. Ramana Maharshi, *Collected Works*, ed. Arthur Osborne (London: Rider & Co., 1959).
2. Quoted in Wilhelm Fraenger, *The Millennium of Hieronymus*

Bosch: Outlines of a New Interpretation, trs. Eithne Wilkins and Ernst Kaiser (Chicago: University of Chicago Press, 1951).

3. Paul Reps, ed., *Zen Flesh, Zen Bones: A Collection of Zen and Pre-Zen Writings* (New York: Doubleday & Co., 1961).

4. Thomas Merton, *The Way of Chuang Tzu* (New York: New Directions, 1965).

5. *Ibid.*

6. Swami Prabhavananda and Christopher Isherwood, trs., *The Song of God, Bhagavad-Gita,* with an introduction by Aldous Huxley (Hollywood: Marcel Rodd Co., 1944).

7. *Ibid.*

8. Dante, *The Divine Comedy, Paradiso,* XXXIII, 143-45, tr. Dorothy L. Sayers.

9. Douglas E. Harding, *The Hierarchy of Heaven and Earth: A New Diagram of Man in the Universe* (New York: Harper & Brothers, 1957).

10. Arthur J. Arberry, *Tales from the Masnavi,* Unesco Collection of Representative Works: Persian Series (London: George Allen & Unwin, 1961.

11. Idries Shah, *Tales of the Dervishes: Teaching Stories of the Sufi Masters over the Past Thousand Years* (London: Jonathan Cape, 1967).

12. Anagarika Govinda, *Foundations of Tibetan Mysticism* (London: Rider & Co., 1969).

13. Farid al-din Attar, *The Conference of the Birds: A Sufi Allegory Being an Abridged Version of Farid-uddin Attar's Mantiq-ut-Tayr,* tr. R. P. Masani (London: H. Milford, 1924).

14. Quoted in Karlfried Graf von Durkheim, *The Japanese Cult of Tranquility* (London: Rider & Co., 1960). This passage echoes the same idea in a very different language.

15. Quoted in Evelyn Underhill, *Practical Mysticism* (London: Jonathan Cape, 1914).

16. Ajit Mookerjee, *Tantra Art: Its Philosophy and Physics* (New Dehli: Ravi Kumar, 1966).

17. Aleister Crowley, *Magick in Theory and Practice by the Master Therion (Aleister Crowley)* (New York: Castle Books, 1960).

18. Daisetz T. Suzuki, Erich Fromm, and R. de Martino, *Zen Buddhism and Psychoanalysis* (New York: Grove Press, 1963).

19. John Heider (Ph.D. diss., Duke University, 1968).

20. Arthur Deikman, "Deautomatization of the Mystic Experience," *Psychiatry* 29 (1966): 324-38.

21. Daisetz T. Suzuki, *The Training of the Buddhist Zen Monk* (Kyoto: The Eastern Buddhist Society, 1934).

22. Isshu Miura and Ruth Fuller Sasaki, *The Zen Koan* (New York: Harcourt, Brace & World, 1965).

23. Daisetz T. Suzuki, *The Field of Zen*, ed. Christmas Humphreys (London, The Buddhist Society, 1969).

24. Idries Shah, *The Sufis* (Garden City, N.Y.: Doubleday & Co., 1964).

25. R. Simac, "In a Naqshbandi Circle," *New Research on Current Philosophical Systems* (New York: Octagon Books, 1968).

26. Martin Lings, *A Moslem Saint of the Twentieth Century* (London: George Allen & Unwin, 1961).

27. Cyprian Rice, *The Persian Sufis* (London: George Allen & Unwin, 1964).

28. *Ibid.*

29. Israel Regardie, *The Tree of Life: A Study in Magic* (New York: Samuel Weiser, 1969).

30. *Ibid.*

31. Quoted in David Krech, Richard S. Crutchfield, and Norman Livson, *Elements of Psychology* (New York: Alfred A. Knopf, 1969).

32. Quoted in Regardie, *op. cit.*

33. Shah, *supra*, note 24.

34. *Writings from Philokalia, on the Prayer of The Heart*, trs. E. Kadloubovsky and G. E. H. Palmer (London: Faber & Faber, 1951).

35. *Ibid.*

36. Durkheim, *op. cit.*

37. William H. Sheldon, *The Varieties of Temperament: A Psychology of Constitutional Differences* (New York: Hafner, 1969).

38. Govinda, *op. cit.*

39. *Ibid.*

40. Erwin Rousselle, "Spiritual Guidance in Contemporary Taoism," *Papers from the Eranos Yearbooks: Spiritual Disciplines*, Bollingen Series XXX No. 4 (New York: Pantheon Books, 1960).

41. Govinda, *op. cit.*
42. *Ibid.*
43. *Ibid.*
44. Edward Conze, *Buddhist Meditation*, Ethical and Religious Classics of East and West, No. 13 (London: George Allen & Unwin, 1956).
45. *Ibid.*
46. *Ibid.*
47. Mircea Eliade, ed., *From Primitives to Zen: A Thematic Sourcebook in the History of Religions* (New York: Harper & Row, 1967).
48. Rouselle, *op. cit.*
49. Dante, *op. cit., Inferno*, I, 16-18.
50. Regardie, *op. cit.*
51. Shah, *supra*, note 11.
52. Friedrich Heiler, "Contemplation in Christian Mysticism," *Papers from the Eranos Yearbooks: Spiritual Disciplines*, Bollingen Series XXX No. 4 (New York: Pantheon Books, 1960).

CHAPTER 3.

1. I. K. Taimni, *The Science of Yoga* (Adyara, Madras: Theosophical Publishing House, 1965).
2. In Trevor P. Legget, *The Tiger's Cave* (London: Rider & Co.).
3. Friedrich W. Nietzche, *Thus Spoke Zarathustra* (Chicago: Henry Regnery Co., 1957).
4. Gama Chen Chi Chang, *The Practice of Zen* (New York: Harper & Brothers, 1959).
5. Shrinyu Suzuki Roshi, a lecture in *Wind-Bell*, Vol. V, No. 3 (1966).
6. Suzuki, *loc. cit.*, Vol. VII, No. 3-4 (1968).
7. Perhaps the best exposition of this is by Sayadow's disciple, Nyaponika Thera, *The Heart of Buddhist Meditation* (London: Rider & Co., 1969). Other good sources are Mahasi Sayadaw, *The Progress of Insight* (Kandy, Ceylon: Buddhist Publishing Society); and Nanomoly Thera, *Mindfulness of Breathing* (Kandy, Ceylon: Buddhist Publishing Society, 1964).
8. Nyaponika Thera, *op. cit.*

9. *Ibid.*

10. The interested reader may find more of its rationale and application in Claudio Naranjo, *The Attitude and Practice of Gestalt Therapy* (to be published by Science and Behavior Books); and in Joen Fagan and Irura L. Sheperd, eds., *Gestalt Therapy Now* (Palo Alto, Calif.: Science and Behavior Books, 1969).

CHAPTER 4.

1. Haridas Chaudhuri, *The Philosophy of Meditation* (New York: Philosophical Library, 1965).

2. Chang, *op. cit.*

3. Kapleau, *op. cit.*

4. Quoted *ibid.*

5. Mircea Eliade, *op. cit.*

6. Quoted *ibid.*

7. Quoted in *Encyclopedia of Religion and Ethics,* ed. James Hastings, *s.v.* "Possession" (New York: Charles Scribner's Sons, 1908-1927).

8. Carl T. Jung and C. Kerenyi, *Essays on a Science of Mythology,* rev. ed. (Princeton: Princeton University Press, 1963).

9. Andreas Lommel, *Shamanism: The Beginning of Art* (New York: McGraw-Hill, 1967).

10. Shah, *Tales of the Dervishes.*

11. Julian Silverman, "Shamanism and Acute Schizophrenia," manuscript in preparation.

12. See Aubin, *Cruel Effets de la Vengeance du Cardinal Richelieu, ou Histoire des Diables de Loudun* (Amsterdam: 1716), quoted in T. K. Oesterreich, *Possession, Demoniacal & Other, Among Primitive Races in Antiquity, the Middle Ages, and Modern Times* (New Hyde Park, N.Y.: University Books, 1966).

13. Mentioned in *Trance and Possession States,* ed. R. Prince (R. M. Burke Memorial Society).

14. Henry Corbin, *Creative Imagination in the Sufism of Ibn" Arabi,* tr. R. Manheim (Princeton: Princeton University Press, 1969).

15. See my discussion of this point in *The One Quest,* Chapter IV: "The Question of Identity."

16. References to the techniques are widely scattered through Jung's

work. The interested reader might consult the thematic indexes to Jung's work.

17. Robert Desoille, *The Directed Daydream*, tr. Frank Haronian, P.R.F. Issue No. 18 (New York: Psychosynthesis Research Foundation, 1966). This was a series of lectures delivered by Desoille at the Sorbonne and published originally in the Bulletin of La Société des Recherches Psychothérapiques de Langue Française (1965).

18. Claudio Naranjo, "Psychotherapeutic Possibilities of Fantasy-Enhancing Drugs," manuscript in preparation.

19. Harold A. Abramson, ed., *International Conference on the Use of LSD in Psychotherapy and Alcoholism* (Indianapolis: Bobbs-Merrill Co., 1966).

20. Alan Watts, *Psychotherapy East and West* (New York: Pantheon Books, 1961). Watts has devoted his book to the parallels between the modern and traditional ways of liberation.

21. Idries Shah, *The Way of the Sufi* (London: Jonathan Cape, 1968).

22. Anita M. Muhl, *Automatic Writing* (New York: Garrett Press, 1964).

23. The essay appeared in the 1910 volume of *Annalem der Naturphilosophie* and was published as a book in 1912.

24. Heinrich Zimmer, "On the Significance of the Indian Tantric Yoga," *Papers from the Eranos Yearbooks: Spiritual Disciplines*, Bollingen Series XXX No. 4 (New York: Pantheon Books, 1960).

25. Quoted in Oesterreich, *supra*, note 12.

26. *Ibid.*

27. Zimmer, *op. cit.*

28. Signe Tokskvig, *Swedenborg, Scientist and Mystic* (New Haven: Yale University Press, 1948).

29. *Ibid.*

30. *Ibid.*

CHAPTER 7.

1. N. W. N. Sullivan, *Beethoven: His Spiritual Development.* (New York: Vintage Books, 1960, pp. 3–4.

Bibliography

This is a selected bibliography of introductory reading on some of the matters discussed in this book.

Behanan, Koovor T. *Yoga: A Scientific Evaluation*. New York: Dover Publications, 1939.

Journal of Transpersonal Psychology (P.O. Box 4437, Stanford, Calif. 94305) carries very good articles on the psychology of mysticism, meditation, physiological feedback, and related matters. The Spring 1970 issue contains an excellent bibliography on meditation, compiled by Beverly Timmons.

Kapleau, Philip, ed. *The Three Pillars of Zen: Teaching, Practice, Enlightenment*. Boston: Beacon Press, 1965.

Lefort, Raphael. *The Teachers of Gurdjieff*. London: Gollancz, 1966.

Luce, Gay. *Time in The Body*. New York: Pantheon Books, 1971.

Ouspensky, P. D. *In Search of the Miraculous*. New York: Harcourt, Brace & World, 1949.

Rahula, Walpola. *What the Buddha Taught*. New York: Grove Press, 1959.

Tart, Charles. *Altered States of Consciousness*. New York: John Wiley & Sons, 1969. (Many of the articles referred to in the Notes are reprinted in this book. An excellent source book.)